Hiker's Guide
to the
Mountains
of
Vermont

D1516955

Hiker's Guide
to the Mountains
of
Vermont

Jared Gange

To Kyla —
Come to Vermont so we
can do Camel's Hump
again!

Jerry

Sept. 2001

Huntington Graphics
Burlington, Vermont

Third edition, August 2001
Printed in Canada

Gange, Jared
    Hiker's Guide to the Mountains of Vermont
    Includes index.
    ISBN 1-886064-12-1

Editing: Linda Young
Graphic design, maps, and typesetting:
  John Hadden, Resting Lion Studio
University of Vermont student interns:
  Jason Evans, Vanessa Price, and Brian Schneider

Please read before using this book:

Hiking, like many outdoor endeavors, is a potentially dangerous activity. Participants in these activities assume responsibility for their actions and safety. No guide book can replace good judgment on the part of the user. Obtain the necessary skills and inform yourself about potential dangers before taking part in outdoor recreation activities. Neither the author nor publisher, nor anyone associated with this book, has any responsibility or liability for anyone who uses the information contained herein or who participates in the sport of hiking. Hike difficulty ratings, time estimates, or impressions are subjective and will vary from hiker to hiker depending on such things as ability, experience, confidence, or physical fitness. As a result, the author cannot assure the accuracy of the information in this book, including hike descriptions, maps, and directions. These may be unintentionally misleading or incorrect.

Also note that access to hiking areas may be changed or revoked at any time. Hikers must be aware that publication of this book does not grant them permission nor a right to use the land on which the hikes mentioned in this book are located. Please obey posted signs that indicate a change in ownership or status of a trail or activity area.

Front & back cover photos: J. Gange
(Inset photo of Camel's Hump by Louis Borie)
Photo facing page: Summit of Mount Mansfield (the Chin) from the Forehead by J. Gange

Hiker's Guide to the Mountains of Vermont

- The 100 best mountain hikes

- All the major summits

- Guide to backcountry skiing

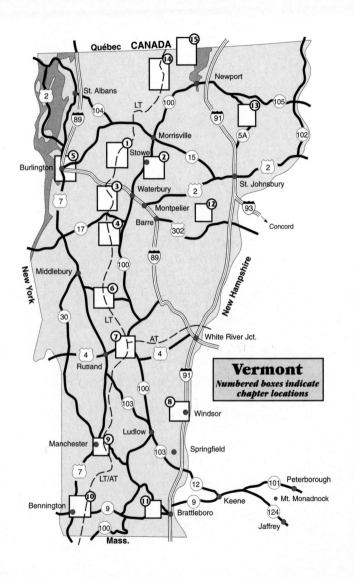

Vermont
Numbered boxes indicate chapter locations

Québec **CANADA**

Newport

St. Albans

Burlington

Morrisville

Stowe

Waterbury

Montpelier

Barre

St. Johnsbury

Concord

Middlebury

New York

Rutland

White River Jct.

New Hampshire

Windsor

Ludlow

Springfield

Manchester

Peterborough

Mt. Monadnock

Keene

Bennington

Brattleboro

Jaffrey

Mass.

Contents

Introduction

The hundreds of miles of trails that wind through the mountains of Vermont — the Green Mountain State — have been enjoyed by hikers for many years. The terrain varies from gentle paths through hardwood forests to steep, rocky scrambles leading to breezy summits. We have tried to make this guide book easy to use by basing the chapters around familiar towns and mountains and presenting the popular hikes for these areas. The detailed maps that accompany the route descriptions show the hiking terrain and the driving approaches to the trailheads. Beginning with the Mount Mansfield region — our most important hiking area — we present the most commonly done hikes from the Camel's Hump, Worcester Range, Mad River Valley, Middlebury, Killington, Manchester, Bennington, Mount Snow, Brattleboro-Putney, Mount Ascutney, Groton State Forest, Northeast Kingdom, and Jay Peak areas. A brief introduction to mountains just across the border in Québec is provided, along with several important hikes in neighboring New Hampshire and Massachusetts.

Our focus here is on mountain hikes, that is, climbing up mountains, usually to the top, but always to a view or something of interest, such as a pond or a cabin. Rather than providing a list of all hiking trails in the state, or an arbitrary selection of hikes, our goal here is to offer the hiker a comprehensive, authoritative selection of hikes throughout Vermont. The previous edition presented 85 hikes; this edition brings the number to an even 100.

In Vermont, hiking information traditionally has revolved around the Long Trail, the "footpath in the wilderness", which runs from the Massachusetts border, north to the Canadian border. Because of this traditional focus on the Long Trail, the Green Mountain Club's early guide books concentrated on the Long Trail. Later the Green Mountain Club brought out a second guide book addressing the other trails in the state, i.e. trails not connected to the Long Trail. Since the vast majority of hiking today is day hiking, and since the day hikes turn out to be both on the Long Trail (Mount Mansfield, Camel's Hump, Mount Abraham, for example) and off the Long Trail (Mount Hunger, Stowe Pinnacle, Mount Ascutney, Mount Pisgah, for example), there would seem to be a need for a guide book that treats the day hiking in Vermont in a systematic fashion. The *Hiker's Guide to the Mountains of Vermont* fills that need: It covers the classic hikes, the highest mountains — by most routes — and local favorites.

Hikers often give themselves long term, or long distance, hiking goals. This usually takes one of two forms: hiking the entire length of a trail, such as the Appalachian Trail, or climbing all the mountains on an established list, such as the 48 mountains over 4,000' in New Hampshire, the traditional 46 peaks in New York's Adirondacks over 4,000', or, most ambitiously, all 4,000' summits (114) in the Northeast. While long-distance hiking might be regarded by some as unimaginative drudgery, and peak-bagging an arbitrary pursuit, both goals are great motivators and encourage us to go places and experience things we otherwise would not. Here in Vermont, the best-known hiking goal is the 265-mile Long Trail. Most hikers do it section by section, usually taking a number of years to complete the entire trail. The *Hiker's Guide to the Mountains of Vermont* provides another option for a hiking goal: Do all 100 hikes in this book and you truly will have hiked Vermont!

Hiking times and distances

In the mountains, it is *walking time* rather than distance travelled that can give us a reliable measure of the actual effort needed to do a particular hike. A three-mile hike in gentle terrain obviously is going to take much less effort than a three-mile hike up Camel's Hump, which requires almost 2,000' of climbing. In the hike descriptions provided, round trip time, round trip distance, and approximate elevation gained are provided, with the time given first. Actual times will vary a great deal from hiker to hiker, or from day to day depending on trail (and hiker) condition. The times provided are determined partly by observation and partly by applying the standard formula of 2 miles per hour plus one half hour per 1,000' gain in elevation. Most hikers should find these time estimates reasonable — some will find them too low, some too high. By providing a *consistent* time rating, hikers using this guide should eventually be able to reliably plan the amount of time they will need for a given hike.

When travelling in the mountains, especially on longer, more ambitious hikes, the main comment about time has to be: Allow extra! It is up to you to build flexibility into your schedule so your group has the leeway to deal with any unplanned events or delays.

In some areas, trails are showing signs of overuse, and in other areas fragile vegetation is at risk. Please respect any signs — trail detours or requests not to walk off the trail, for example — that you might encounter. In fact, during the spring mud season, about mid-April to Memorial Day, many of the trails are closed. This is because of the much greater damage done by boots when trails are soft and muddy.

Hikers on the summit ridge of Mt. Mansfield   David Seaver

Getting started

Most of the routes in this book will be enjoyable for hikers of all levels of experience, and most can be done at a reasonable pace in a half day or less. Round trip times and distances are given for each hike, and difficult trail sections are noted. To get started, begin with the shorter hikes in your area. Find out what sort of footwear works for you and get an idea of how *your* normal hiking pace compares with the times given here. You probably already have done some form of hiking or extended walking, and the role of this guide is to enable you to discover Vermont's popular hikes. For those not comfortable with the do-it-yourself approach, there are organized hiking trips; these are noted in local newspapers. Here in Vermont, the Green Mountain Club (GMC) is the primary hiking organization. If you are a regular user of hiking trails, consider joining or supporting the GMC or your local hiking club. The Green Mountain Club has over a dozen local chapters, making the Club accessible throughout the state.

Hiking Guidelines

- Pick a route that is within your group's ability.
- Allow yourself plenty of time.
- Let someone know your plan, then stick to it.
- Exercise extra caution if hiking alone.
- Pack out what you pack in.
- Pets should be controlled at all times: on a leash near water sources and on summits above tree line.
- Take water/drinks with you. The Giardia parasite is widespread, so it is best to play it safe.
- Respect owner signs and private property.

Always take extra clothing: preferably something that will keep you dry *and* protect you from wind. Before starting out, remember there is always the possibility that the weather will deteriorate during your trip. Be prepared for this! The variability of weather is especially a concern for early summer and fall hikes, as even on fine days, the summits are cooler and breezier than the valleys below.

There is great variation in hiking abilities and tastes, and this in turn makes it difficult to give general advice on clothing and equipment. For example, work out what footwear works best for you by trying different options and by consulting your nearest outdoor outfitter. A number of Vermont's hiking and backpacking suppliers are represented in this guide. In part, this recognizes the essential role they play in advising and educating the public about appropriate and cost-effective footwear, packs, parkas, and accessories. But they are also a source of local hiking information and current trail conditions. Some of them have assisted with the selection of hikes for this guide book. They are presented in the "Sponsors" section.

Maps

Complete topographic map coverage for Vermont, and the rest of the country as well, is provided by the United States Geological Survey (USGS). Currently there are three available map formats. The most widely used is the 7.5-minute series with a scale of 1:24 000. In a few areas these have been replaced by the new 1:25 000 metric format (7.5 by 15 minutes, with twice the area). Both formats display information at a very detailed level, and hiking trail information is reasonably up to date. However, note that some of the 7.5-minute quadrangles were prepared more than 30 years ago and therefore may not show all roads or current trailheads. A 1:100 000 scale metric series (1 degree of longitude by 30 minutes of latitude) is also available. Although these maps lack the detail of the two series mentioned above, they are very useful in gaining an understanding of a larger area, a county, for example. Major hiking trails are shown, and the contour interval is 20 meters. Both metric map styles come folded, with a cover, as opposed to the loose sheet style of the non-metric series. The excellent 15-minute series (1:62 500) has been discontinued by the USGS.

The Vermont Atlas and Gazetteer (by DeLorme) or *Vermont Road and Atlas Guide* (by Northern Cartographic) are very useful in navigating back roads and finding trailheads; these map books provide a good level of detail. In addition to the above atlases, excellent regional hiking maps are now available for many areas in Vermont. These are noted at the end of hike descriptions under "Maps".

1 | Mount Mansfield Region

As the highest mountain in Vermont, and the dominant landmark in the Burlington area, Mount Mansfield (4,393') naturally receives a great deal of attention from hikers. The Long Trail traverses its 2-mile, open summit ridge, and there are nine hiking routes up the mountain. A gondola and a toll road to the summit ridge make the upper mountain accessible to everyone. The following pages describe the main routes up Mount Mansfield, as well as some nearby hikes: Sterling Pond, Elephant's Head, and Whiteface Mountain. Two areas to the south of Mansfield, Nebraska Notch, and Bolton Valley, also are included in this chapter.

1 Long Trail route up Mount Mansfield

The popular route from the Stowe side follows the Long Trail south (actually west) from Route 108. This excellent trail climbs steadily and steeply through woods, reaching **Taft Lodge** (caretaker in summer) after 1.7 miles and about 1.5 hours. From here, the trail is rougher and steeper, breaking into the open about 10 minutes past Taft. The exciting final section to the summit is up steep rocks. Although it is not really difficult, use caution, especially if the rocks are wet. The 360-degree view from the summit is spectacular. Return by the same route, or, for a route more protected from the elements, continue south from the summit on the Long Trail (LT) for 0.2 mile and turn left on the **Profanity Trail**. It uses a steep gully to descend directly to Taft Lodge, returning you to the Long Trail.

5 hours and 4.7 miles round trip. Elevation gain: 2,800'
Approach: From Stowe, go west on Rt. 108 for 8.5 miles, passing the ski area entrances and park at the Long Trail.
Maps: *Northern Vermont Hiking; 20 Day Hikes in the Mount Mansfield Region*

Aerial view of the Chin   Ed Rolfe

2 Hell Brook Trail

One of the most continuously steep and rough trails in Vermont, Hell Brook is not recommended for beginners. However, many experienced hikers (and expert powder skiers) will want to do this challenging trail. Not advised for the descent, and especially not when it is raining! After its long and arduous climb, the trail breaks into the open upon reaching the summit ridge, about 1.3 miles from the road. (**Hell Brook Cut-off Trail** branches left to **Taft Lodge** at 0.9 mile.) Head left to reach the Long Trail and follow it to the summit — only 1.8 miles from the road. The recommended descent route is via the **Long Trail** and Taft Lodge, leaving you with an easy 0.9-mile road walk (left) back to Big Spring.

4 hours and 5 miles round trip. Elevation gain: 2,600'
Approach: From Stowe, drive up the Mountain Road past the ski resort to Big Spring, 9 miles from Stowe and VT 100. Hell Brook Trail is 150' up the road on the left.

3 The Gondola and the Cliff Trail

Another relatively expedient way up Mount Mansfield is to ride the ski area's gondola and then hike the remaining 0.7 mile to the summit. The gondola ends a few hundred feet below the summit ridge, and once the summit ridge is reached, it is an easy walk to the top. The problem is getting to the ridge; the **Cliff Trail** is quite difficult in a few places and involves sections of steep climbing up some large boulders. Head right (south) 150' from the gondola to pick up the Cliff Trail. Once on the ridge, head right (north) on the **Long Trail** for the remaining 15 minutes (0.4 mile) to the top. Note this trail junction for your return. An easier and longer descent route is as follows: From the top, head down the Long Trail the way you came, but stay on the open summit ridge (1.4 miles) to the **Toll Road**. Then continue down the Toll Road and turn left onto the first ski run, the **Nosedive**. Follow this and other ski runs down the mountain, returning to the base station and completing the loop.

3-4 hours and 4 miles total. (Descend via ski trails.)

Approach: The base station of the gondola is 7.5 miles from Route 100 in Stowe, on Route 108.

4 The Nose (4,062') via the Haselton Trail

Angling up to the left from the base of the gondola (approach as above), the Haselton Trail climbs at a pleasant angle, crossing several ski trails before merging with **Nosedive** (ski run) and ending on the **Toll Road** (at 1.6 miles) just below the Octagon restaurant. Follow the Toll Road (right) 0.5 mile to the **Summit House** on the summit ridge. From here a 0.2-mile scramble on the **Triangle Trail** leads to the top of the impressive peak. Descend same route.

3-4 hours, 4.6 miles total. Elevation gain: 2,500'

Aerial view of Mount Mansfield summit ridge   Ed Rolfe

5 The Toll Road up Mount Mansfield

Starting from the Toll House on the Mountain Road, 6 miles from Stowe, the gravel-surfaced Toll Road climbs to the summit ridge of Mount Mansfield in 4.5 miles. From here, it is an easy and spectacular 1.4-mile hike north along the Long Trail to the **Chin**, Mount Mansfield's summit. Most drive up the Toll Road, but it is open to hikers at no charge. Once on the summit ridge, hikers are reminded to stay on the actual trail (or rock outcroppings) as the fragile arctic-alpine vegetation is damaged easily by foot traffic. The **Nose** (4,062'), the mountain's southern summit, looms above the parking area, and a short hike (20 minutes) brings you to its top. There are excellent views of the summit ridge for many miles in all directions. Guide books and maps can be purchased at the **Summit Station**, located at the top of the Toll Road.

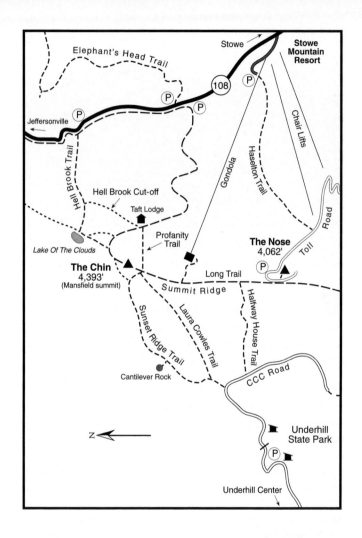

18 Mount Mansfield

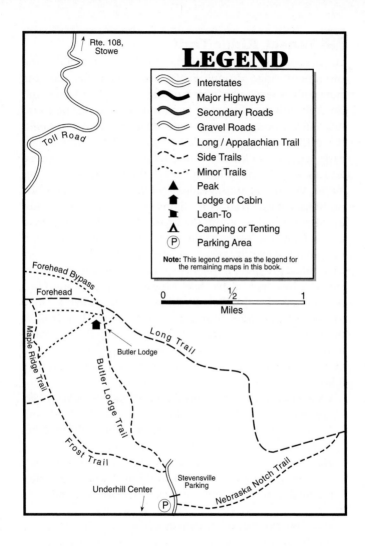

↑ Rte. 108,
Stowe

LEGEND

〰〰	Interstates
〜	Major Highways
〜	Secondary Roads
〜	Gravel Roads
‑‑‑	Long / Appalachian Trail
‑ ‑ ‑	Side Trails
····	Minor Trails
▲	Peak
⬟	Lodge or Cabin
◼	Lean-To
ⒶΔ	Camping or Tenting
Ⓟ	Parking Area

Note: This legend serves as the legend for the remaining maps in this book.

0   ½   1
Miles

Toll Road

Forehead Bypass

Forehead

Maple Ridge Trail

Long Trail

Butler Lodge

Butler Lodge Trail

Frost Trail

Stevensville Parking

Underhill Center

Ⓟ

Nebraska Notch Trail

6 Sunset Ridge Trail

On the west side of Mount Mansfield, Sunset Ridge is the prominent ridge dropping off the summit. Because the ridge offers sweeping views of the Champlain Valley and the Adirondacks, this route is considered one of the finest hikes in Vermont — many would say *the* finest. Accordingly, it is often somewhat crowded, so you might want to get an early start on weekends. From Underhill State Park (nominal fee), ascend the moderate grades of the **CCC Road** for about a mile, where the Sunset Ridge Trail branches left. Continue on **Sunset Ridge Trail** as it climbs steeply through woods, eventually coming out on the broad, open ridge. From here to the **Chin** (the summit) the route is out in the open, and the grand westerly views of the Adirondacks and Lake Champlain are quite impressive, especially in late afternoon sun. The low-angle slabs make for easy but fun hiking. On a hot summer day, make sure you have plenty to drink. Once on the summit ridge, bear left (north) on the **Long Trail** to the summit, 0.2 mile farther on. After enjoying the panoramic views, and the various ski lifts and runs on the other side of the mountain, descend by the route you came, carefully following the signs.

5 hours and 6.6 miles round trip. Elevation gain: 2,550'
Approach: From Underhill (Route 15), drive to Underhill Center. Continue to Mountain Road, a short distance beyond and follow it to Underhill State Park.
Side trail: About 0.7 mile above the CCC Road, a short (0.1-mile) spur trail leads left to the well-known **Cantilever Rock**, a rock that juts about 25' out over the trail.

Maps for the Mount Mansfield Region: 20 Day Hikes in the Mt. Mansfield Region; Northern Vermont Hiking

Sunset Ridge on Mansfield, from Underhill   Jared Gange

7 Laura Cowles Trail

From Underhill State Park, walk up the CCC Road. After about a mile, the Laura Cowles and Sunset Ridge trails branch left off the road. Then, after 0.1 mile, Laura Cowles Trail branches right. It ascends very directly to the summit ridge, at times climbing stone stairs before rejoining the Sunset Ridge Trail just west of the Long Trail. The views on Laura Cowles are very limited until near the top. Take the Long Trail for the final 0.2 mile to the summit. The best descent route is via the open Sunset Ridge, thus you "walk into the view" as you hike down. This loop combination is a good variation on the Sunset Ridge Trail route.

5 hours and 6 miles round trip. Elevation gain: 2,550'

8 Halfway House Trail

South of Laura Cowles, the Halfway House Trail also ascends Mansfield's west flank, but it offers better views than the Laura Cowles Trail. As for Laura Cowles and Sunset Ridge, start from Underhill State Park but continue on the CCC Road 0.2 mile past the Sunset Ridge turnoff. Here the Halfway House Trail branches off left and ascends to the summit ridge and the LT after 1.1 miles of very steep climbing. At the Long Trail, head left for 1.2 miles to the summit of Mansfield. The usual descent route would be via Sunset Ridge as this returns you to Underhill State Park. Thus this route is analogous to the Laura Cowles-Sunset Ridge loop, but it is somewhat longer.

5-6 hours and 6.8 miles round trip. Gain: 2,550'

Approach: From Underhill Center, drive to Underhill State Park. Start out as for Sunset Ridge.

Hiker nearing the summit of Mt. Mansfield   David Seaver

9 Maple Ridge

Sunset Ridge and Maple Ridge are the two main west ridges of Mount Mansfield. Maple Ridge descends from the Forehead (the southernmost summit) towards Underhill Center. From the parking area at the end of Stevensville Rd., take the **Frost Trail** to **Maple Ridge Trail**. Continue up the ridge (the trail name changes to **Wampahoofus Trail**) to the **Forehead's** open summit at 3,940'. This route has some rather difficult sections — including a short cliff and a crevice jump — making it one of the most exciting trails in Vermont! The views constantly change as the trail works its way across huge slabs and around improbable rock formations. From the Forehead, either descend the way you came, follow the Long Trail (south/right), or continue (north/left on the LT) to the Nose or the Chin. To descend south from the Forehead, follow the Long Trail right, passing over exciting, somewhat challenging terrain involving several ladders. Note: This route is not suitable for dogs. After 0.8 mile, branch right (side trail) to **Butler Lodge**. From here, continue down to Stevensville Rd. An easier descent option from the Forehead is to use the weather-protected Forehead Bypass (east of the LT), a pleasant route on much easier terrain through a cool and mossy birch wood. It rejoins the LT a few minutes before you reach the link to Butler Lodge.

5 hours and 5.5 miles round trip. Gain: 2,550'
Maple Ridge-Forehead-Butler Lodge loop:
5 hours and 5 miles round trip. Gain: 2,550'
The Nose is 0.8 mile farther, the Chin, 2 miles.

Approach: From Underhill Center, drive to the end of Stevensville Road and park. Walk up the (gated) road, taking the Frost Trail (left) 0.2 mile from the car.

A steep section on Maple Ridge   Susan Ross

10 Maple Ridge - Sunset Ridge Loop

This is a fine, if rather vigorous, way to climb Mount Mansfield — call it the deluxe route from the west. From Underhill State Park, follow the gravel **CCC Road** about a mile to where the Sunset Ridge Trail branches off left. (There is a marked shortcut trail that cuts across the CCC Road several times and is an alternate route to this junction.) Bear right and continue along the road, which degrades into an unimproved track. The trail makes a gradual uphill climb while crossing several small brooks before coming to the **Maple Ridge Trail**. From the sign, the trail climbs steeply over smooth rocks before emerging onto Maple Ridge. The trail becomes increasingly steep in this section with several jumps and vertical climbs. (Great views now!) Upon reaching the **Forehead** of Mansfield, bear left on the **Long Trail** across several bog puncheons before reaching the TV road. The LT bears left on the road before re-entering the woods on the right and soon comes to the Mt. Mansfield Visitor Center. (An ascent of the **Nose** (4,062'), Mansfield's south summit is highly recommended. The 0.2-mile **Triangle Trail** ascends steeply to the top.) Continue along the spectacular, open **summit ridge** for about a mile and a half, eventually reaching the junction with the Sunset Ridge Trail. Here keep right and make the short climb (0.3 mile) to the **Chin**, Mansfield's summit. From the summit, retrace your steps to the junction to pick up **Sunset Ridge Trail**. It descends the moderate slabs of Sunset Ridge: wide views to the west. Below tree line, the trail descends steeply (it can be slippery and rough in places) and then more moderately, passing a junction with the Cantilever Rock spur trail. From here it is a short descent to the CCC Rd. and Underhill St. Park.

6 hours and 8 miles. Elevation gain: ca. 2,950'

11 Long Trail to Sterling Pond

This extremely popular hike leads to a pleasant mountain pond and, a short distance away, a sweeping view north from the top of a ski run. From **Smugglers Notch** (2,612'), take the well-maintained Long Trail north as it climbs fairly steeply and steadily. Bear left at the pond for a short distance to reach the ski area viewpoint. Sterling Pond Shelter and Watson Camp are 0.3 mile farther on. Descend by the same route. (See Elephant's Head Trail)

2 hours, 2.2 miles round trip. Elevation gain: 930'

Approach: Park at (the top of) Smugglers Notch on Route 108, 10 miles from Stowe and 8 miles from Jeffersonville.

12 Elephant's Head

This difficult and varied hike leads to a spectacular ledge 1,000' above Smugglers Notch. From the south end of the picnic area, cross the stream, then ascend very steeply (for 20 min.), soon crossing a landslide ravine (good views). From here, the trail is intermittently quite rough. It skirts the edge of the steep mountainside (a cliff), but the dense forest gives a feeling of security, while only partially obscuring the dramatic views of Mansfield. A spur trail (0.1 mile) descends very steeply to dramatic Elephant's Head ledge. *Note:* The spur trail might be closed during the summer months to protect Peregrine Falcon nesting. Return by the same route, or continue to Sterling Pond and on down to Smugglers Notch via the Long Trail (longer).

3 hours and 4.4 miles (up and back). Gain: 1,500'

Approach: Park at the Smugglers Notch picnic area on Route 108, above the entrances to the Stowe ski area: it's on the right, a short distance beyond the Long Trail.

13 Long Trail Traverse of Mount Mansfield

The 10-mile traverse of the long ridge of our highest mountain from Lake Mansfield to Smugglers Notch is one of Vermont's most rugged and spectacular hikes. Sweeping views, an exciting 2 miles of trail above treeline, and some difficult climbs make this a memorable outing. The trip is done in either direction and with variations. To reach the trailhead for **Taylor Lodge**, drive to the end of Nebraska Valley from Stowe. Hike in past the Lake Mansfield Trout Club (private) and walk over easy terrain before climbing steeply to the lodge (space for 20) and the Long Trail at 1.6 miles. After avoiding **Nebraska Notch** proper (a jumble of huge boulders), the LT traverses the west flank of Dewey Mtn., passing **Twin Brooks tenting area** 2 miles from Taylor Lodge and reaching the side trail left to **Butler Lodge** 1.3 miles farther on. Butler (space for 14) is perched nicely, high on the mountain. The next day return to the Long Trail and ascend the exposed slabs of the **Forehead** (use protected Forehead Bypass in bad weather). From the top of the Forehead, it is 2 miles to the **Chin** (main summit), most of which is along the open summit ridge. On the way, an ascent of the **Nose** is recommended. The Triangle Trail ascends the steep rocks to the top: 0.2 mile. Now walk the long, gentle summit ridge to the mountain's highest point. After enjoying the views, descend to **Taft Lodge** either via the somewhat exposed LT (0.4 mile), or if the weather is bad, backtrack (0.2 mile) to the **Profanity Trail**, which drops (left) directly down to Taft. From the lodge down to Route 108, it is a pleasant 1.7 miles.

Distance: 10.7 miles, climbing: 4,000' Time: 1-2 days
USGS maps for Mansfield: USGS Mt. Mansfield 1:100 000 (metric) and Mt. Mansfield 1:24 000

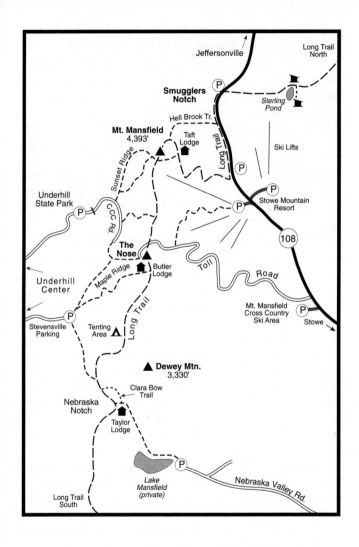

14 Nebraska Notch (1,850') from the east

From Lake Mansfield Trout Club (private), traverse north of the lake, then up a steep section to **Taylor Lodge** and the **Long Trail**, where there are limited views over Nebraska Valley. Return by the same route. From Nebraska Notch, it is 6 rugged miles north on the Long Trail to the top of Mount Mansfield via the Forehead, the Nose, and the summit ridge.

2.5 hours and 3 miles round trip. Gain: 750'

Approach: From Route 100, just south of Stowe, drive through Moscow to the hiker parking lot just below the Trout Club, at the upper end of Nebraska Valley.

15 Nebraska Notch from the west

From Stevensville parking, the Nebraska Notch Trail leads off to the right. After climbing gently through an open forest, the trail descends to cross a footbridge before making a brief climb to reach the **Long Trail** at 1.5 miles. Continue on the LT south (0.7 mile down past beaver ponds, then a steep climb) to **Taylor Lodge**, which is located just off the LT (left). The 0.4-mile **Clara Bow Trail** tackles the wild, boulder-filled ravine of Nebraska Notch proper and provides a fun, challenging loop variation to Taylor Lodge. Head left 0.3 mile past the LT junction and thread your way past huge rocks, trees clinging to cliffs and through a cave-like grotto with a ladder exit. A beaver pond with commanding views of the notch appears on your left just before Taylor Lodge.

3 miles (1.5 to the LT, 2.2 to Taylor Lodge) and 2-3 hours round trip. Elevation gain: 520' (Same for the loop.)

Approach: From Underhill Center, take Pleasant Valley Road 0.2 miles north and turn east (right) on to Stevensville Road. Pass the winter parking area (on the left) and continue to the parking area at 2.8 miles.

Beaver lodge in Nebraska Notch   Jared Gange

16 Dewey Mountain 3,330'

There is no maintained trail up this steep, densely forested mountain. The Long Trail stays well below the summit. Seen from the east or from Maple Ridge Trail on Mansfield, Dewey's sharp form is intriguing. Although not the shortest way, the route from the Mt. Mansfield Ski Touring Center is perhaps the easiest to describe. Following ski trails from the Ski Center, reach the Burt Trail (ski trail) and follow it to Dewey Saddle on Skytop Ridge. The upper section of the Burt offers a beautiful climb through old-growth forest with huge paper birches. From the small saddle, climb right, finding the best route you can. It should take you about 30 minutes to bushwhack to the heavily forested summit. Climb a tree to fully appreciate the excellent view! Return by the same route.

17 Whiteface Mountain 3,715'

The pointed summit of this steep-sided peak yields good views if you move through and around the trees. Whiteface also is referred to as Sterling Mountain, and the compact group of summits northeast of Smugglers Notch is known as the Sterling Range. From the car, walk in on a woods road for 2 miles (blue blazes) to where the **Whiteface Mountain Trail** turns off to the right. It climbs steadily, reaching **Whiteface Shelter** and the Long Trail after a mile. Bear right 0.4 mile on the LT, which climbs steeply to the summit. Descend by the same route, or, for a good loop hike, continue south on the Long Trail past the Whiteface Trail junction, over **Morse Mountain**, past **Hagerman Lookout** to **Chilcoot Pass**, in the saddle below **Madonna Mountain** (This is Smugglers Notch Ski Area). From here, head left and descend extremely steeply 0.8 mile to **Beaver Meadow Lodge**. Keep left to return to the road used on the way in.

Vegetation Above the Tree Line

In Northern Vermont a phenomenon known as the tree line occurs at about 4,000' of elevation. Above this height, mainly because of lower average temperatures, trees do not thrive. While the transition from spruce-balsam forest to open mountainside can vary somewhat depending on the local "micro climate", it is quite abrupt when it does happen. Thus hikers can find themselves suddenly very exposed to the elements upon emerging from the protection of a dense forest onto a wind-blasted summit ridge. The brief transition zone is home to gnarled and wind-stunted trees called krummholz.

However, the above-treeline area is far from lifeless. A large variety of grasses, sedges, mosses, and flowers make their home in this "arctic-alpine" zone. The name is appropriate because our high mountain plants are also present in the sub-arctic latitudes of Labrador and Alaska. Some areas in the Northeast — the Alpine Garden on Mount Washington (New Hampshire), for example — are famous for their spring (June at this altitude) displays. Because the above-treeline areas in Vermont are extremely limited in size (a few summits), they receive a heavy concentration of hiker traffic. And because of the short growing season, and the plants' precarious existence generally, visitors must exercise extreme care not to step on or sit on any plants. Please leash your dogs and make sure everyone walks only on rock slabs or gravel areas.

Loop: 5 hours and 8.7 miles. Total elevation gain: 2,400'
Approach: From Morristown Corners (north of Stowe), head west on Walton Rd., then *south* on Cole Hill Rd. At 2 miles, turn right on Mud City Rd. At 4.4 miles, turn left on Beaver Meadow Rd. Park in the clearing at 5.8 miles.

18 Ricker Mountain 3,401'

From the ski area base lodge, ascend the ski slopes under the Number 2 chairlift, then follow the service road to the top of Number 4 chair. From here, continue past the top of the lift and find the path that leads to the wooden observation tower. The views are excellent, especially of Camel's Hump. Descend by the same route.

2 hours and 2 miles round trip. Elevation gain: 1,400'
Approach: Drive to the Bolton Valley Ski Area. The 4-mile access road leaves Route 2 six miles west of Waterbury. From Burlington, use the I-89 Richmond exit and Route 2.

19 Bolton Mountain 3,725'

The isolated, rounded shape of this relatively high but viewless mountain is a prominent part of the landscape as seen from I-89 and Burlington. From Bolton's ski touring center, hike up the George's Gorge and Raven's Wind ski trails, eventually reaching the Long Trail. Continue (right) for about 0.7 mile to the top. Descend by the same route.

About 3.5 hours and 5 miles round trip. Elev. gain: 1,800'

20 Harrington's View 2,520'

For a shorter, and probably more interesting hike than the above, start from the Ski Touring Center and walk out Broadway to Bobcat. At the top of Bobcat, continue to Eagle's Nest, and from there, hike up to the Long Trail. Harrington's View, an open rock ledge with a nice view, is then about 20 minutes to the south (left). Return on the same trails.

2 hours, 3 miles, elevation gain: 500'
Approach: As above, drive to Bolton Valley Ski Area.

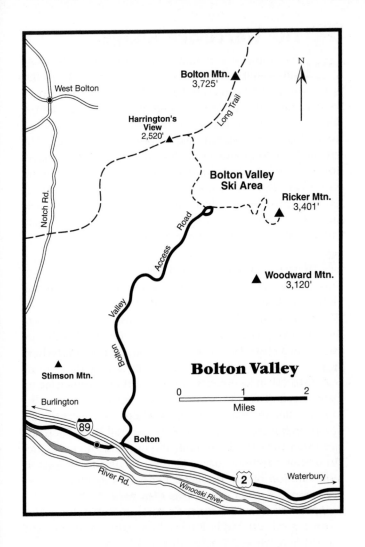

N

Bolton Mtn.
3,725'

West Bolton

Harrington's
View
2,520'

Long Trail

Bolton Valley
Ski Area

Ricker Mtn.
3,401'

Notch Rd.

Access Road

Woodward Mtn.
3,120'

Valley

Bolton

Stimson Mtn.

Bolton Valley

0   1   2
Miles

Burlington

89

Bolton

River Rd.

2

Waterbury

Winooski River

2 | The Worcester Range

The impressive mountain wall that parallels Route 100 from Waterbury north past Stowe to Morrisville is known as the Worcester Range. High above Waterbury Center, the major hiking destination of the range, Mount Hunger is plainly visible — it is the bare, rounded knoll, just to the right of a slightly higher point on the ridge. The Skyline Ridge Trail runs along this ridge from Mount Hunger north to Hogback Mountain and continues to Mount Worcester. North of Hogback Mtn., the trail forks with the left fork dropping steeply to merge with the Stowe Pinnacle Trail, which then leads down to Stowe Hollow. The right fork continues north to Worcester Mountain.

21 Mount Hunger 3,538'

This classic hike affords some of the best mountaintop views in Vermont: Camel's Hump looms to the south, Waterbury Reservoir is below, and Mt. Mansfield beckons to the northwest. The White Mountains of New Hampshire are visible on a clear day. From the parking area, the **Waterbury Trail** ascends through woods, gradually at first, then steadily and steeply in its upper section — at times clambering up giant "steps". The trail breaks into the open just below the top. Be sure to note your surroundings as you enter the open summit area in order to find *your* trail back. There are two other trails off the summit and currently no trail signs. On a sunny summer day, relax and enjoy this hospitable mountain top. Mount Hunger is known for its blueberries.

> *4 hours, 3.8 miles round trip. Elev. gain: 2,290'*
> *Approach:* From Waterbury Center, just east of Route 100, drive north on Maple Street, then right on Loomis Hill Road. Stay left at 2.7 miles. Park at 3.7 miles.

View from Mount Hunger   David Seaver

Just below the summit of Mount Hunger, the trail to **White Rock Mountain** (3,194') branches right. This rough trail leads to the interesting open rocks on White Rock Mountain, including a huge, level rock slab below the summit. The trail then heads around to the east side of the mountain and ends on the **Middlesex Trail** (east side route) about a mile below the top of Mount Hunger. Head left and make the steep, enjoyable climb to the summit. This longer variation is well worth it if you are up for the extra hour or two.

22 Mount Hunger from Middlesex

Somewhat longer than the Waterbury route, the **Middlesex Trail** is the standard route from the Montpelier area. It is a more varied trail than the Waterbury route, and the upper section negotiates a series of interesting slabs. This route is not recommended when conditions are icy! The signage leaves something to be desired, but the blue-blazed trail is excellent and recommended as a change for those who usually climb Mount Hunger from the Waterbury side. At 1.5 miles, the **White Rock Trail** branches to the left (sign). Because there are two other trails off the top, note the route carefully as you approach the summit to avoid confusion on your descent. Mount Hunger's views are among the best. Camel's Hump, Mount Mansfield, Waterbury Reservoir, and the mountains of New Hampshire: All are in plain view.

4 hours and 5.6 miles round trip. Elevation gain: 1,900'
Approach: From Montpelier, drive north on Route 12 to Shady Rill Road and turn left. After 2.2 miles, turn right on Worcester Road for 0.7 mile, then left for 1.8 miles to a clearing and the parking area.

23 Stowe Pinnacle 2,740'

A great hiking goal for families, the top of the Pinnacle has superb views and plenty of space for hikers to spread out and relax. This very popular, moderately strenuous hike starts out as a gentle climb (often somewhat muddy), before gradually getting steeper and rockier. The **Pinnacle Trail** levels off briefly in a saddle — a short spur trail leads left to a lookout over Stowe and Mt. Mansfield — then descends steeply a short distance before climbing to the dramatic open summit. Stay right at the (possibly unmarked) junction of the **Skyline Ridge Trail** (to Mount Hunger and Waterbury)

Stowe Pinnacle   Jared Gange

about 0.2 mile below the top. From the rocky summit dome
there is an unobstructed view of Stowe and its western wall
of mountains. The view extends from Camel's Hump in the
south to Jay Peak in the north, with the Worcester Range
directly above. Descend by the same route. For a longer variation, see the Skyline Ridge Trail on page 39.

2.5-3 hours and 3 miles round trip. Gain: 1,520'

Approach: Take Goldbrook Road (1.5 miles south of
Stowe on VT 100); at 0. 3 mile, turn left. At 1.8 miles turn
right onto Upper Hollow Road and park on the left at 2.3
miles, in the marked hiker parking lot.

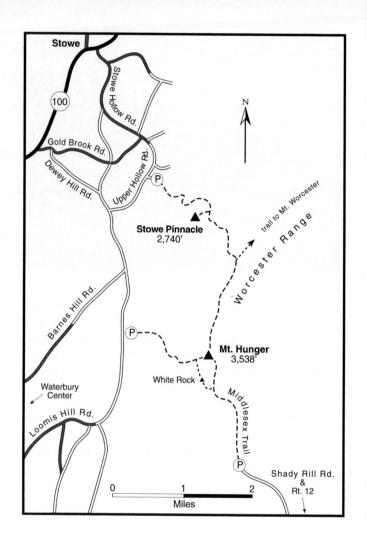

40 Worcester Range

24 Skyline Ridge Trail

This relatively new and as yet little-used trail seems to be slowly gaining acceptance. To do the standard ridge traverse, climb Mount Hunger from the Waterbury Center side (This is more convenient for car shuttling than from the Middlesex side.). From the summit of Hunger, head left (north), and follow the blue-blazed trail as it works its way along the ridge over the north summit of Hunger and past Hogback Mountain. The high point of the ridge is 3,642'. There are occasional outlooks along the way. After about 2 miles, the trail descends steeply (stay left at a trail junction) to **Stowe Pinnacle**. From the **Pinnacle Trail** junction, it is only a 0.2-mile detour (left) to the wide-open top of Stowe Pinnacle (dramatic views) and 1.3 miles on down to Stowe Hollow. This challenging hike, over steep and rough terrain, offers an alternative to the area's heavily used trails. A longer version of this ridge walk is to bear right at the (upper) trail junction, about 2 miles beyond Hunger. This follows the main ridge for about 3 miles to the summit of **Mount Worcester** (3,293'). From here it is 2.5 miles down the Worcester Mountain Trail to Worcester. The village of Worcester is on VT Route 12, north of Montpelier.

In the future: The Dept. of Forests, Parks and Recreation plans to continue the Skyline Ridge Trail north to Mount Elmore.

4-6 hours and 7 miles, one way. Elevation gain: 2,900'
(Mt. Hunger-Stowe Pinnacle-Stowe Hollow)

Approach: Same as for the trail up Mount Hunger from Waterbury Center, via Loomis Hill Road.

Maps: *Northern Vermont Hiking; 20 Day Hikes in the Mount Mansfield Region; USGS 1:100 000 Mount Mansfield; USGS 1:24 000 Stowe*

Green Mountain Club Hiker Center

Vermont's primary hiking and backpacking organization, the Green Mountain Club (GMC), has its headquarters on Route 100 in Waterbury Center, about 4 miles north of Waterbury and Interstate 89. The club's **Gameroff Hiker Center** sells various maps and guide books, and there are displays and photos of interest to hikers. GMC staff members are on hand to answer questions and help you with trip planning. The hiker center is open daily from Memorial Day to Columbus Day. In the off-season, the adjacent club office is open during regular business hours, and hikers are always welcome. Lectures and workshops are held at the hiker center; these generally are open to the public. Ask for a schedule of upcoming events.

Sign for the Gameroff Hiker Center at GMC Headquarters
Dave Seaver

25 Mount Worcester 3,293'

Mount Worcester is probably the least-visited of the Worcester Range peaks, but it offers a fine hike to an open summit. The **Skyline Ridge Trail** now connects Mount Worcester to Mount Hunger and to Stowe. Perhaps Mount Worcester will see more visitors as a result. The existing trail climbs the mountain from the Worcester side, i.e. from the east. It ascends steadily, for the most part at quite a pleasant angle, reaching the broad, rocky summit after 2.5 miles. Descend by the same trail.

3.5 hours and 5 miles round trip. Elevation gain: 1,970'
Approach: From the village of Worcester (on Route 12, north of Montpelier), drive up Minister Brook Road 1.5 miles to Hampshire Road and turn right. At 3.9 miles, turn left and park at 4.1 miles.

26 Mount Elmore 2,608'

Although it is the lowest of the Worcester Range peaks described here, Mount Elmore is noticed immediately from most vantage points in the Stowe-Morrisville area because of its isolated position at the end of the ridge. The peak is very prominent from the Trapp Family Lodge, for example. Climb the tower on the summit for great views of the lake, nearby farms, Mount Mansfield, and the mountains to the north such as Belvidere and Mount Pisgah. From the state park, follow the blue-blazed trail (it starts out as a service road) for about 2 miles to the open summit. Descend by the same route. Near the top, a half-mile spur trail leads to **Balanced Rock**, a worthwhile addition to the basic hike.

2.5 hours and 4.2 miles round trip. Elev. gain: 1,450'
Approach: From Morrisville, drive north 4 miles on Route 12 to Lake Elmore State Park. Nominal fee charged.

3 Camel's Hump

One of Vermont's best known landmarks, Camel's Hump (4,083') offers possibly the finest mountain top in the state. Unspoiled by roads, ski areas, and communication antennas, its compact, rocky summit floats high above Burlington and the Champlain Valley. The Adirondacks are 50 miles to the west across Lake Champlain; the White Mountains of New Hampshire define the eastern horizon, and the Green Mountain chain stretches to the north and south.

27 From the west: the Burrows Trail

This popular route from Huntington represents the closest route for those coming from Burlington. From the parking lot, the well-maintained Burrows Trail immediately enters a hardwood forest, climbing moderately and steadily. The trail is more difficult higher up, with a prolonged steep and rocky section starting at about 1.5 miles. The slope slackens shortly before intersecting the Long Trail (2.1 miles) at a small clearing, 0.3 miles from the top. This is a good spot to eat, relax, and put on more clothes if descending hikers report windy or cool conditions on the summit. From the clearing, turn right (south) on the **Long Trail** and scramble up the final very steep rocks, coming out into the open just below the summit. This last section is dramatic, as you suddenly emerge from dense woods to huge views of the Champlain Valley and the Adirondacks. Once on the summit the panoramic view — in fair weather — will test your mountain identifying skills for a good while. You might want to continue down below the summit to find secluded spots: This is a busy place on good weather days. Descend by the same route or do the loop variation, as described next.

Camel's Hump from Huntington   Louis Borie

4 hours and 4.8 miles round trip. Elevation gain: 1,950'
Approach: From Richmond (exit 11 on I-89), drive south 9 miles through Huntington to Huntington Center. Turn left on Camel's Hump Road and follow it 3.5 miles to the end.

Forest City Trail variation: Immediately after starting out on the Burrows Trail, turn right onto the short connector trail to the **Forest City Trail**. Here head left and climb up to **Wind Gap** on the LT at 1.4 miles. **Montclair Glen Lodge** is just to the right, and the top is north (left) along a demanding and very interesting 2-mile section of the LT. The final portion is spectacular, offering a fun scramble (traverse left) along the base of the summit cliff before the final climb on easy slabs to the summit. Descend by the Burrows Trail. This is a great way to do Camel's Hump: it's a classic!
5 hours and 6 miles round trip. Elevation gain: 2,400'

28 From the east: the Monroe Trail

Probably the most popular route up Camel's Hump, the Monroe Trail (formerly Forestry Trail) is the natural route for those coming from the east. A wide, comfortable trail, especially in the first mile, it passes the **Dean Trail** at 1.3 miles and higher up, crosses the Alpine Trail at 2.5 miles. (The Alpine Trail traverses the east flank of the mountain, from near Gorham Lodge to a point on the Long Trail at the base of the cliffs on the mountain's south side.) After 3.1 miles, the Monroe Trail ends on the Long Trail, at the clearing just north of the summit. The Burrows Trail, approaching from the west, ends here also. Now head south (left) on the Long Trail for 0.3 mile up steep and rocky terrain to the bare summit. For many, this is the best mountain top in the state. If it's breezy on top, you can usually find shelter behind a rock outcropping. Descend the same route: LT off the summit, then right on the Monroe Trail.

4 hours and 6.8 miles round trip. Elevation gain: 1,800'

Approach: From Waterbury (I-89, exit 10), take Rt. 2 through Waterbury, turn right on Rt. 100, and then immediately right again onto River Rd. Follow it 4 miles, then turn left and continue (climbing) for 3.5 miles to the parking area.

Dean Trail variation: 1.3 miles up the Monroe Trail, the **Dean Trail** branches left to **Wind Gap** and the Long Trail. From Wind Gap, head right on the **Long Trail** for 1.7 miles to the top. The trail is quite steep and rough just above Wind Gap, followed by an easy section, before a prolonged steep climb up to the base of the final cliffs which are skirted to the left. (The scant remains of a plane wreck (1940s) can be seen a short way down the **Alpine Trail**.) The final climb up summit slabs makes for a great finish.

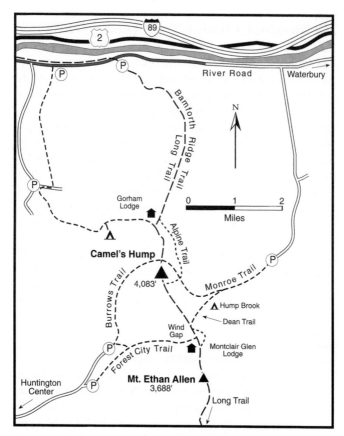

Descend north on the Long Trail, turning (right) down the **Monroe Trail**, 0.3 mile below the top. The loop offers more variety and more walking than the simple up-and-down.

About 5 bours, 7.5 miles. Elevation gain: 1,800'
Maps for Camel's Hump: Northern Vermont Hiking and 20 Day Hikes in the Mt. Mansfield Region

29 Bamforth Ridge Trail (Long Trail)

Although it receives a fraction of the traffic of the Burrows and Forestry Trails, the Bamforth Ridge Trail is in excellent condition. Starting at an elevation of only 350', it climbs steadily, at times quite steeply, to gain the top of the steep northern end of Bamforth Ridge. After about 1.5 hours, you reach the first of several open, ledgy sections with good views of the Hump and vistas to the east and west. From here, the trail takes on a more undulating character, crossing numerous open areas with good views. The final stiff climb of over 1,000' takes you past the **Alpine Trail** to **Gorham Lodge** (3,400') and on to the summit, 0.9 miles beyond Gorham Lodge. Descend by the same route or by one of the other trails.

7-8 hours, 11.8 miles round trip. Elevation gain: 4,000'
Approach: Cross the Jonesville bridge (US 2, east of Richmond) and drive east (left) on River Road for 3.5 miles (past the Long Trail) to the small parking area on the left.

30 Mount Ethan Allen 3,680'

Ethan Allen is the peak just south of Camel's Hump. Ethan Allen does not rise above treeline, but it does offer some good views, especially north to Camel's Hump. From the Huntington side, hike up the Forest City Trail to the Long Trail (2.2 miles). **Montclair Glen Lodge** is a hundred yards or so south on the Long Trail. From here it is one mile and 1000' of climbing (at times steep) to the summit of Ethan Allen.

4 hours, 6.4 miles round trip. Gain: 1,600'

Ethan Allen from Camel's Hump   Jared Gange

Skier at Wind Gap, south of Camel's Hump   Jared Gange

Winter Activity on Camel's Hump

In recent winters, hikers and backcountry skiers have been very active on the mountain. The Burrows, Monroe, Forest City, and Dean trails all seem to receive regular attention from skiers and snowshoers. It is frequently possible to hike quite pleasantly on a packed trail to the top of Camel's Hump in the middle of winter.

Telemarkers enjoy the steep slopes on the east side of the mountain, especially off the Alpine Trail. The Forestry/Dean Trail route to the beaver pond below Wind Gap is a favorite among snowshoers.

Coming from the south, the **Catamount Ski Trail** traverses the west side of the mountain at a low elevation (1,500') before descending north-facing **Honey Hollow** to meet the Long Trail for the final section down to River Road.

Outdoor winter activity in northern New England, especially at higher elevations or in remote locations, requires a significantly greater level of preparation and conditioning than trips over the same terrain in the summer. There are various factors to consider: The days are much shorter (i.e. early darkness); there is a potential for rapid deterioration in conditions (drop in temperature, strong winds, reduced visibility, changing snow conditions); and it is generally more difficult to find and follow trails in winter. Perhaps the most surprising difference between summer and winter is the extreme variability of winter conditions... What was easy and fun last week, or just an hour ago, can turn into a very serious undertaking.

4 The Mad River Valley

Home of the Sugarbush and Mad River Glen ski areas, the "Valley" offers good hiking, including two or three classic Vermont trips. In particular, the section of the Long Trail between Lincoln Gap and Appalachian Gap is something most hikers will want to do. This sharply-defined, at times quite narrow, 11-mile ridge includes Mount Abraham, Mount Lincoln, Mount Ellen, and the top of Mad River Glen, thus it crests all three ski areas. Waitsfield and Warren are the two towns in the Mad River Valley.

31 Mount Abraham 4,006'

The lowest of Vermont's five mountains over 4,000', Mount Abraham just barely pokes above the tree line. It is a great trip for kids who are up for 4 to 5 hours of hiking. For many kids, Mount Abe is the first "real" hike. From Lincoln Gap, follow the **Long Trail** north over varied terrain, passing **Battell Shelter** at 1.7 miles and reaching the summit at 2.6 miles. At the Battell Shelter, the Battell Trail joins from the left: It originates in Lincoln. The final section of the trail is steeper in spots and involves a little easy scrambling up rock slabs. Once on the top, the superb view is known for giving a sensation of peering straight down on the farms of Lincoln. Needless to say, this is a fantastic spot during fall foliage.

4 hours and 5.2 miles round trip. Elevation gain: 1,700'
Approach: From Warren, drive up Lincoln Gap Road, and park in one of several parking lots just below the height of land in Lincoln Gap. From the west, drive to Lincoln and follow the Lincoln Gap highway to the Gap.

Mount Abraham from Lincoln   Dave Seaver

32 Sunset Ledge

This short, out-and-back hike south on the Long Trail from Lincoln Gap requires about 40 minutes of walking each way. The ledges are just off the trail to the right. This is a dramatic spot with great views of Lincoln, and in the distance, the Adirondacks. The hike has some steep sections in the beginning but is easier higher up.

1.5 hours and 2 miles round trip

Approach: Drive to Lincoln Gap from Warren or Lincoln. The Lincoln Gap Road is very steep and winding and is closed for the season as soon as snow falls.

33 Mount Abraham via the Battell Trail

The route up Mount Abraham from the Lincoln side is somewhat longer and involves more climbing than from Lincoln Gap, elevation 2,410'. The trail climbs surprisingly moderately over its 2-mile length and ends on the Long Trail, just south of **Battell Shelter**. From here, continue north on the Long Trail to the summit. The trail breaks into the open just below the top. Return by the same trail. The arctic grasses and other vegetation that grow at the summit area are damaged easily by foot traffic and regenerate very slowly. Therefore, hikers are asked to keep off the grass!

5 hours and 5.8 miles round trip. Elevation gain: 2,550'
Approach: From Lincoln, drive north on Quaker St. for 0.5 mile, turning right on Elder Rd. Follow signs to trailhead.
Map: USGS Lincoln

Dead fir trees near tree line   David Seaver

34 Jerusalem Trail up Mt. Ellen (4,083')

This is a fine west-side approach, similar to the Battell Trail on Mt. Abraham. From the car, follow the trail for 2.5 miles to the ridge and the Long Trail. The trail is gentle in its lower section, then steepens as it nears the Long Trail. From here it is 1.8 miles (right) to the top of Mt. Ellen, and the 0.2-mile spur trail to **Glen Ellen Lodge** is just to the north. It is 1.7 miles north to the top of the single chairlift at Mad River Glen (good views).

5-6 hours, 8.6 miles round trip. Elevation gain: 2,580'

Approach: From Rt. 116, drive 3.3 miles up Route 17 and bear right on Jerusalem Rd., then left on Jim Dwire Rd. at 4.6 miles. The trailhead is on the right after 0.5 mile.

Moss Glen Falls, near the Mad River Valley   David Seaver

35 Lincoln Gap to Appalachian Gap

Between these two gaps, or mountain passes, the crest of the Green Mountains forms a sharp ridgeline that keeps a high elevation. The Long Trail runs along the ridgecrest: this section of the LT is a classic. Although the ridge is generally densely wooded, the trail itself is challenging, and there are enough viewpoints to make this a very worthwhile excursion. It can be done in a single day by fit hikers. Others may want to spread the trip over two days. From Lincoln Gap, at 2,410 feet, take the **Long Trail** north past the **Battell Shelter** (room for eight sleepers) to the summit of **Mount Abraham** (4,006'). A comfortable time for this first portion is 2 hours. From here, it is 2 miles to the top of **Sugarbush Ski Area** (Castlerock Lift). Continuing along the narrow, forested ridge, cross the top of **Mount Ellen** (4,083') and the **Sugarbush North Ski Area** (excellent views) after about 4 hours of walking and 6.5 miles. (If it is necessary to cut the trip short, descend to the base of the ski area.) After descending from Mount Ellen, pass the Jerusalem Trail on the left, and at 8 miles, the short spur trail (right 0.3 mile) to **Glen Ellen Lodge** (space for 8). A mile farther on, you reach the top of **Mad River Glen Ski Area** and **Stark's Nest**, a rustic building that has been refurbished recently, from which there are good views. From here it is 2.5 miles over relatively easy terrain to Route 17 in Appalachian Gap.

7-8 hours, 11.6 miles. Elevation gain northbound: 2,520'
Approach: Start from Lincoln Gap or Appalachian Gap. Appalachian Gap is on Route 17, 6 miles west of Waitsfield. Route 17 is kept open year round.

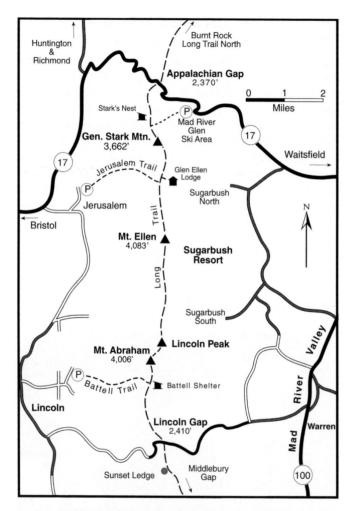

Maps: *USGS Lincoln, Mt. Ellen, Waitsfield, Huntington, Montpelier (1:100 000 metric)*

36 Mad River Glen Ski Area and General Stark Mountain (3,662')

The goal here is to climb up the ski runs to the top of Mad River Glen's legendary single chairlift. This is the lift on your left, as seen from the base of the ski area. There are only a few lifts here, so it is possible to hike out of sight of cables and lift towers. There are beautiful large maples and birches, and the woods are well-groomed, creating the effect of a steep park. At the top of the lift (3,644'), there is an old, but refurbished building (**Stark's Nest**), with a deck that is a good place to relax and enjoy the view. Mad River's runs are very steep, and there are occasional cliffs, thus it is a good idea to take it easy when descending. Take the ski run just south of the top when starting down. General Stark Mountain is a short (0.6 mile, 20 minutes) walk south on the Long Trail and is slightly higher than Stark's Nest.

3-4 hours, 3-4 miles round trip. Elevation gain: 2,000'
Approach: From Waitsfield, drive west on Route 17 to the large parking area at the base of Mad River Glen Ski Area.

Giant White Trillium   David Seaver

37 Burnt Rock 3,160'

This rolling trail climbs through creeks and hardwood forest, connecting with an old road and then following it up the valley. Big rock croppings are abundant as the trail climbs, turns south, and then levels out to reveal good views of Burnt Rock summit (on the right). The **Hedgehog Brook Trail** then steepens for a short time before connecting with the Long Trail, which winds through softwoods. The trail heads steeply up here; the rocks and hemlocks make this section interesting. The trail then opens up with various views on the way to the summit with its panoramic views.

3 hours, 5.2 miles. Elevation gain 1,090'

Approach: From Waitsfield drive north on VT 100 for 3.4 miles then turn left on to North Fayston Road. Continue straight at Big Basin Road (7.5 miles). Reach parking area at 8.4 miles. The trail begins on the left.

Is the Water Safe To Drink?

When you are hot and thirsty, it's hard to resist a sparkling brook. Used to be you could drink water safely from streams and rivulets. But today, with the **Giardia lambia parasite** — a widespread microscopic organism — the recommendation is to treat all drinking water. One option is to boil it for about five minutes. Another is filtering; be sure to have the correct kind of filter. Iodine and chlorine treatments are poor options, as they don't destroy the parasite.

The symptoms are nasty: diarrhea, gas, stomach cramps, weight loss, and nausea. They can be with you for months even years, so this isn't something to take lightly! Animals and people pass the parasite through feces, thus hikers should bury waste at least 200' from any water source.

5 | Burlington

Vermont's largest urban area happens to be located near some of the state's best hiking: Mt. Mansfield, Camel's Hump, and Mount Hunger. But there are good hiking and walking areas within the greater Burlington area itself. Shelburne's Mount Philo is a classic short hike, and the gentle, open terrain of Shelburne Farms offers some of the finest walking anywhere.

38 Eagle Mountain 574'

Spectacular views of Lake Champlain reward the hiker for trekking up the gentle backside of this lakeside bluff. Milton's **Eagle Mountain Natural Area** has a well-marked trail network, and the easy terrain makes the hikes accessible to all ages. A combination of trails #1 and #2 gets you to both the (wooded) summit and clifftop Hoyt Overlook with views of Lake Champlain and South Hero. Cedar Island and Fishbladder Island lie below, while the rugged Adirondacks define the western horizon.

Loop: 1 hour and 1.8 miles. Total elevation gain: 400'
Approach: From Burlington, drive north on I-89 to exit 17 and head west on US2 for only 0.3 mile (from the interstate overpass) before turning right on Jasper Mine Road. Turn left, and at 0.6 mile, turn right onto Mayo Road.

39 Mount Philo 980'

A popular short hike with sweeping views of Lake Champlain and the Champlain Valley, Mount Philo is a moderate little jaunt, although steep. Hikers can choose between the paved road or a somewhat steep and rough trail. From the gate, the trail heads (left) through woods, traversing the west side of the mountain. It ascends moderate-

Mt. Philo from the west   Jared Gange

ly, crosses the road then gets much steeper and switches
back to the south. At the fork (sign) you have the option to
head to Devil's Rock or the summit overlooks. From here
it's not far to the top via the Overlook Trail. The trail comes
out at the western overlook. From there it's only a short distance to the main overlook. Both have excellent views. The
summit area has picnic tables and camping sites, and all visitors are charged a nominal usage fee. Follow the road or
the trail back down to the parking area. Probably because of
the steep and rough nature of the trail, the paved road
seems to be the preferred route for hikers.

1-2 hours and 2.3 miles. Total elevation gain: 350'
Approach: From Burlington take Route 7 south. Philo is a
couple of miles north of North Ferrisburg. Turn east at the
blinking yellow light on to State Park Road. Drive 0.6 mile
to the park gate. At the summit, there is a parking lot.
More parking is available on the road outside the gate.
Map: *Vermont Atlas and Gazetteer, page 38*

40 Lone Tree Hill, Shelburne Farms

Originally a vast farm estate, Shelburne Farms and some of its important buildings are now open to the public. Shelburne Farms has a well-signed trail network. A trail map is included in the nominal entrance fee. This short, introductory walk offers sweeping views with relatively little exertion. The **Farm Trail** begins to the left of the Welcome Center and is marked with blue reflectors on stakes. An easy 15-minute walk brings you to the gigantic **Farm Barn** (shown above), an architectural treasure. The trail passes to the left of the barn and continues 0.3 mile to the top of Lone Tree Hill. From this grassy knoll, the Adirondacks, Lake Champlain, Shelburne Point, and much of Shelburne Farms are yours! It's a great spot for a picnic. Return by the same route or use the map to put together a longer variation. The entire Farm Trail Loop is 4.25 miles.

1 hour and 2 miles. Total elevation gain: 150'

Approach: From Shelburne village on Route 7, head west on Harbor Road 1.5 miles to the Shelburne Farms entrance and Welcome Center. Park here, on the right.

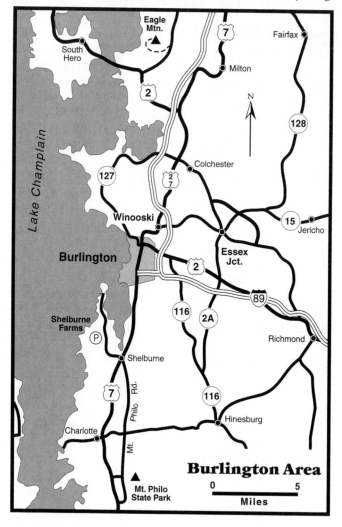

Burlington Area

0   5
Miles

6 Middlebury and Brandon

The hikes for this area are spread around: Snake Mountain rises out of the farming country west of Middlebury; Rattlesnake Point is high above Lake Dunmore; Mount Horrid Overlook is in Brandon Gap; and the Robert Frost Lookout is reached by hiking along the top of Middlebury College's Snow Bowl Ski Area. Last, we give various hikes that use the Long Trail between Middlebury Gap and South Lincoln.

41 Snake Mountain   1,287'

Snake Mountain is a distinctive north-south running ridge of hills that rises almost 1,000' above the farms of Addison County. The views of Lake Champlain and the Adirondacks from the top of the cliffs are beautiful, especially in the late afternoon. From the gate, walk up the pleasant woods road. After a "T" (head left), the route steepens and zig-zags up the mountainside. Once you are on the ridge, watch for the side trail (left) out onto the top of the cliffs, where there is an old foundation. You might see ravens gliding above the line of cliffs. Return by the same route.

2.5 hours and 3.6 miles round trip. Elevation gain: 950'
Approach: From Middlebury, take Route 125 to Route 22A then drive north 4.5 miles to Wilmarth Road. Turn right and continue to the T-intersection with Mountain Road. The trail up Snake begins on the gated woods road right at the intersection, and the trailhead parking is 50 yards left on Mountain Road.
Map: USGS East Middlebury

A raven alights on Snake Mountain　　　　　Jared Gange

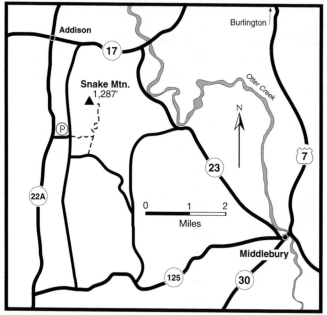

42 Abbey Pond 1,700'

With its marshlands, hemlocks, and birch, Abbey Pond is a lovely spot to have a picnic and relax. You'll find small islands and brush along the edges of the water, giving the pond a cozy feel. The Robert Frost Mountain overlooks the pond and wetlands, which provide habitat for all kinds of wildlife. From the parking area follow the well-marked, blue-blazed trail, which follows an old road. This moderate trail with one steep section crosses a stream bed a few times; you will see cascades as well.

2 hours and 3.8 miles. Elevation gain 520'

Approach: From Bristol, drive south on Rt. 116 for 8.4 miles. A sign on the left (east) directs you to the parking area down a dirt road. Park at the old sugar house.

43 Bristol Cliffs Wilderness

This is a wilderness area just south of Bristol. There are 3,740 acres of forest with cliffs overlooking the Champlain Valley and a couple of ponds and multiple little streams. The Wilderness is a fun place to spend time in the woods away from people. Because this is a wilderness area, visitors must be sure to preserve the natural character of the area and to protect the plant and animal species in their undisturbed habitat. For more information on the Wilderness, the Forest Service has free pamphlets.

Time and distance: variable Elevation gain: 800 - 1000'

Approach: From West Lincoln, a wilderness sign directs you south onto York Hill Road. Drive 1.7 miles to a 10-car parking area on the right. The small footpath soon disappears in the woods.

Maps: USGS South Mtn.; Vt. Atlas & Gazetteer, p. 39

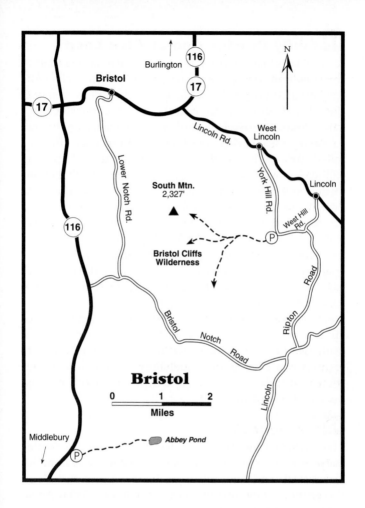

44 Emily Proctor–Cooley Glen Loop

A solid day's hike, this loop is formed by two access trails to the Long Trail and the connecting 5.6-mile section along the trail itself. Although the route is almost entirely wooded, there is a fine, open ledge near the top of Mount Roosevelt called **Killington Overlook**. From the trailhead, take the trail to **Cooley Glen Shelter**, reaching the **Long Trail** after 3.4 miles. Turn right, heading south along the LT, passing Killington Overlook at 7 miles and reaching **Emily Proctor Shelter** at 9 miles. From here, it is 3.5 miles down the Emily Proctor Trail to your starting point. The mountains traversed on this section of the Long Trail are: Mt. Cleveland, Mt. Roosevelt, and Mt. Wilson (at 3,745', the highest).

> *7-8 hours, 12.5 mile loop. Elevation gain: 3,120'*
>
> *Approach:* From Lincoln (east of Bristol), drive through South Lincoln to Forest Road #201 (USFS signs). Turn left and proceed to the trailhead and parking.

To climb **Breadloaf Mountain** (3,835'), hike to Emily Proctor Shelter, then south on the LT for 0.7 mile. A short spur trail to the west leads to good views from this summit, the highest between Lincoln and Middlebury Gaps. (For a shorter route to Breadloaf (7 miles round trip), see the trail description to **Skylight Pond**.)

45 Skylight Pond

The **Skylight Pond Trail** provides quick access to **Skyline Lodge**, a nice cabin nestled above Skylight Pond. Both are just east of the Long Trail. From the parking area, walk up the gentle woods road for about 20 minutes, when it will begin to steepen. After a steady climb, there are views through the trees just before reaching the Long Trail (2.3 miles). Straight on is the trail to the cabin and the pond. To

Falls of Lana   David Seaver

your right (LT south), the spur trail (right) to Battell
Lookout, with good views west, is 250' away. Descend by
the same route.

4 hours, 5 miles, elevation gain: 1,400' (Skyline Lodge)
Approach: From Ripton (east of Middlebury on Rt. 125),
take Forest Rd. #59 (left) 3.6 miles to the trailhead.

46 Robert Frost Lookout

From Middlebury Gap, hike south on the **Long Trail**, passing through the Middlebury College Snow Bowl Ski Area. Ski trails are crossed seven times. Actually, the best views on the entire trip are from the first and last of these ski trail crossings! The first clearing has excellent views to the west, and the last one has good views to the east. After leaving the ski area, the trail steepens, soon reaching Robert Frost Lookout with a view to the west. After passing a few more minor lookouts, you reach the viewless, wooded summit of **Worth Mountain**, 3,234'.

4.5 hours and 5.4 miles round trip. Gain: 1,300'

Approach: From Middlebury, drive to East Middlebury then up Route 125 to Middlebury Gap.

47 Cape Lookout Mountain 3,298'

This hike includes the spectacular views of **Brandon Gap** from popular **Mount Horrid Overlook**. From the parking area, cross the highway, and following the Long Trail north up through a fine birch forest, reach the spur trail (right) to the overlook after about 20 minutes. Walk out on the ledge for the view. *Note:* Because of Peregrine Falcon nesting, access to the top of the cliff might be closed from spring to late summer. Continue on the LT over **Mount Horrid** to the top of Cape Lookout Mountain. There are a couple of interesting viewpoints along the way. Return by the same route.

3 hours, 3.4 miles round trip. Elev. gain: 1,300'

Approach: From Brandon, drive east 8 miles on Rt. 73 to Brandon Gap. Parking is on the south side of Rt. 73. From Rochester (on Rt. 100), Brandon Gap is 10 miles west.

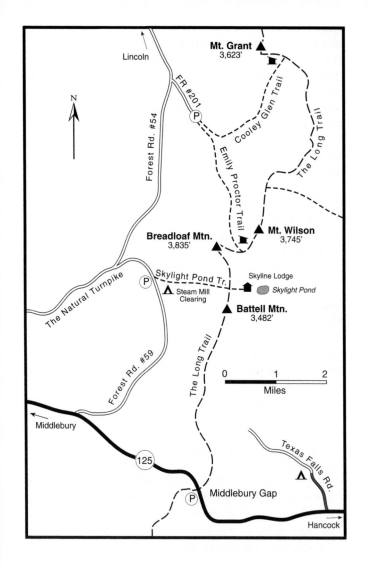

48 Rattlesnake Point

This moderate hike leads to spectacular views of Lake Dunmore and Silver Lake. Not an actual summit, Rattlesnake Point is a group of ledges looming high above the lake. From the popular **Falls of Lana** (only about 15-20 minutes walk), follow signs to Rattlesnake Cliff — it is about 1.6 miles farther on. The excellent trail climbs briskly then eases before climbing very steeply for a short distance to the spur trail, which leads left to the ledge overlooks. Both viewpoints should be visited, although the south lookout has a wider and more varied view. Unlike many precipitous dropoffs, these roomy ledges are inviting places to relax.

3 hours and 4.5 miles round trip. Elevation gain: 1,100'

Approach: A short distance south of the park entrance are two parking areas on the left. Both are trailheads for the Falls of Lana, but the second (farther) one is the main one.

49 Falls of Lana

A nice swimming destination, the soothing sounds of water reward you at the falls with its large pool and dramatic boulders. From the parking loop (on the right) follow an access road along easy grades up to the falls and Silver Lake. You will pass stones and boulders along the route, reaching a clearing with views of Lake Dunmore just before you reach the falls.

15-20 minutes, 1 mile round trip.

Approach: Drive 6 miles north of VT 73 in Forestdale or 3.5 miles east of US 7. Signs mark the parking area on the east side of the road, 0.2 mile south of the Branbury State Park Entrance, on the east side of Lake Dunmore. A short distance south of the entrance are two parking areas on the left. Both are starting points for Falls of Lana.

Lake Dunmore and Branbury State Park

Nestled at the foot of the Green Mountains, between Middlebury and Brandon, Lake Dunmore is a very popular swimming and boating spot. Of the several hikes in the area, Rattlesnake Point offers the best views. The less strenuous hike to peaceful Silver Lake is also a favorite.

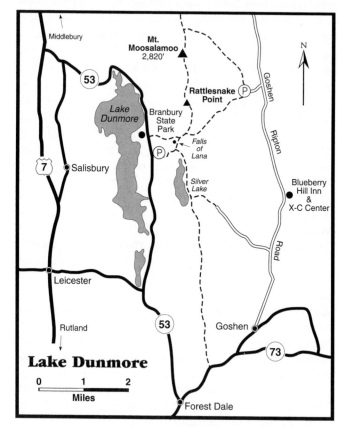

7 Killington and Rutland

Killington Peak, together with its various satellite peaks, is one of Vermont's largest mountains. It is also the home of the East's largest ski area, and the ski trails offer the hiker open slopes with great views. The **Long Trail/Appalachian Trail** passes through here, and just north of busy Route 4, the trails separate — the AT heads east to New Hampshire, and the LT continues north to Canada.

51 Killington Peak 4,241'

The most popular hiking trail up Vermont's second highest mountain is the **Bucklin Trail** (blue blazes), which ascends from the west. The first 2 miles are along a gentle woods road and make for easy walking. After branching (right) off the road, the trail climbs very steeply all the way to **Cooper Lodge** on the Long Trail, slackening only a short ways below the lodge. From here, continue for 0.2 mile (steep) to the open, rocky summit with fine views in all directions, although various antennas clutter the view to the southeast. Descend by the same trail.

5–6 hours, 7.2 miles round trip. Elevation gain: 2,480'
Approach: 5 miles east on Route 4 (from Rt. 7 in Rutland), turn right on Wheelerville Road. Park after 4 miles.

52 Killington ski trails:

From the Killington Base Lodge, hike up under the K1 Express Gondola. As you ascend the very steep, grassy ski run, a fine view gradually unfolds. This "alpine" hiking terrain offers a pleasant change from our typical forest trails.

Time and approach: Drive to the upper end of the Killington Access Road. The hike up will take 1-2 hours. The chairlift is in operation throughout the summer.

Pico Peak from Rutland   Jared Gange

53 Pico Peak 3,957'

Although lower than Killington, Pico's location and attractive symmetrical shape make it more noticeable, especially from the Rutland side. The peak offers good hiking with great views from the summit. Also, Pico is climbed easily by hiking the ski trails. For the Long Trail route, head south from Sherburne Pass. After about 20 minutes, there is a short side trail to the top of a chairlift and a view. At 2.5 miles you reach **Pico Camp**, a small cabin for Long Trail hikers. From here, the **Pico Link** side trail branches right and climbs steeply for 0.4 mile to the top.

4 hours, 5.8 miles round trip. Elevation gain: 1,810'
Approach: From Sherburne Pass at the LT/AT crossing.

54 Deer Leap Rock

The interesting cliffs directly above Sherburne Pass on Route 4 provide a dramatic view of **Pico Peak** and the highway just below. To get to the top of the cliffs, follow the Long Trail and Appalachian Trail north for 0.5 mile to Maine Junction, where the two trails separate. Just beyond, left off the LT, the **Deer Leap Trail** climbs pleasantly through open woods, reaching a junction after 0.4 mile. Head left for 0.2 mile to the viewpoint and then return the same way. At the upper junction, the other fork loops back down to the LT, at a point 1.3 miles from Route 4. Note: For safety reasons, the short and steep scramble up the cliffs has been closed by the Forest Service.

2 hours and 2.2 miles round trip. Elevation gain: 650'
Approach: Park next to the Long Trail Inn at Sherburne Pass on Route 4, about 10 miles east of Rutland.

55 Shrewsbury Peak 3,720'

This eastern satellite peak of Killington offers good hiking in a less-visited area. From the parking area, the blue-blazed **Shrewsbury Peak Trail** makes a short climb then descends briefly before resuming its steady climb to the top. There are no viewpoints along the way but once at the summit you will enjoy excellent views to the south. Descend by the same trail. For a longer variation: From the top of Shrewsbury, it is just a short way to the **Black Swamp Trail**, and about 2 miles on to the Long Trail. The Black Swamp Trail descends (right) for 1.5 miles to Black Swamp Road. It is then about 2.2 miles by road back to the base of the Shrewsbury Peak Trail.

3 hours, 3.6 miles round trip. Elevation gain: 1,500'
Approach: From Rt. 100, 3 miles south of Rt. 4, turn right

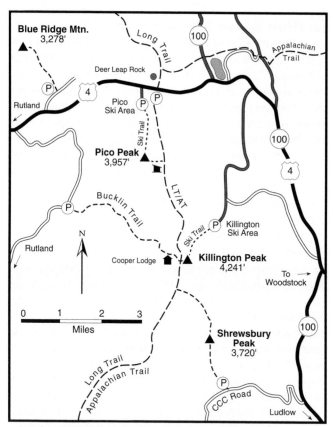

on the CCC Road for 3.3 miles to parking on the right. From the west, the trailhead is 3 miles east of North Shrewsbury.

Maps: *USGS Killington Peak 1:24 000,*
USGS Rutland 1:100 000 (metric),
Vermont Atlas and Gazetteer, p. 29

56 Blue Ridge Mountain 3,278'

Located northwest of Killington and Pico, the rocky summit of Blue Ridge Mountain offers views of Rutland, Killington, and nearby mountains. From Turnpike Road, follow blue blazes along a woods road past a large camp building and onto the **Canty Trail**. The trail is gradual at first, then climbs steeply along a brook for a while before climbing over easier terrain through some nice woods to a clearing and the summit. By continuing a short way beyond the summit, you will be rewarded with better views. Descend by the same trail.

3.5 hours and 4.8 miles round trip. Gain: 1,500'

Approach: About 6 miles east of Rutland, turn left off Route 4 on to Turnpike Road and proceed for 0.7 mile to a gated road on the left. Park on the road shoulder.

Green Mountain National Forest

Vermont's Green Mountain National Forest, our only national forest, comprises 350,000 acres. The northern section runs along the Green Mountains from US Route 4 north to Bristol, while the southern section runs south from Wallingford to the Bennington area. The Forest Supervisor's office is located on Route 7 in Rutland, and district offices are found in Middlebury, Rochester, and Manchester. Each office maintains a Visitor Information Center, which offers free handouts on outdoor activities: hiking, biking, fishing, camping, canoeing, wildlife viewing, cross country skiing, and snowmobiling. Rangers are on hand to answer questions. In Vermont, the Forest Service maintains access roads (Forest Service Roads), campgrounds, and over 500 miles of trails; thus it is an important part of the outdoor recreation picture in Vermont.

Deer Leap Rock from Sherburne Pass Jared Gange

57 Birdseye Mountain 2,216'

Just beyond (east) the parking area, Route 4A crosses a
bridge, and the trail (old road) is to the right in the woods.
Head south to a large clearing and continue on any of several old roads. Before long you will reach another clearing
with power lines. The key to finding the platform is to continue to skirt west (to the right) while ascending the mountain. If it gets too steep and there are cliffs, head more to the
right to find the pocket. On top is an old hang gliding platform with mountain views, including the Adirondacks. This
should be called a bushwack even though a series of old
roads leads almost to the top. Go from road to road in the
correct direction and you will reach the top!

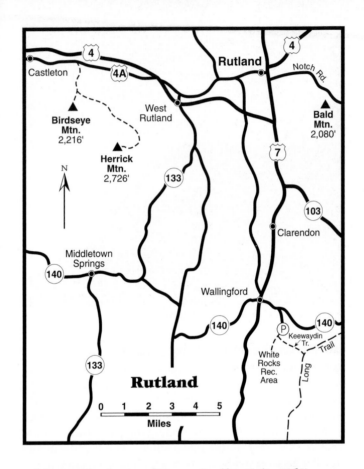

2 hours 15 minutes, distance 3 miles, Gain: 1260'
Approach: Take US Route 4 west from Rutland to exit 5.
From exit 5 (Casleton) on Route 4, follow Route 4A (0.1
mile) east (toward Rutland) to a dirt parking area on the
right (2.9). Travel 2.8 miles on Route 4A.

Bully Brook cascades down the mountain   Jared Gange

58 White Rocks (Ice Bed Trail)

This destination, an area of jumbled boulders where lingering ice creates cool breezes, gives this hike its name. From the southwest corner of the picnic area, follow the blue-blazed trail. After crossing a brook, the path climbs a knoll (0.2 mile). On the left, a spur trail offers a nice view of White Rocks Cliffs, formed by glacial action. After a more expansive view of the cliff area greets you at 0.3 mile, the trail descends and joins a jeep trail. Go left to cross the stream. The Ice Beds, the source of the stream, are 0.5 mile farther.

1.5 hours. 0.3 mile to vista, 0.8 mile to Ice Beds.
Gain: 170' to vista, from the vistas to Ice Beds, -270'
Approach: From the Wallingford Four Corners, head east on VT Route 140. At 2.1 miles bear right and follow signs to White Rocks National Recreation Area.

59 White Rocks Cliffs (Keewaydin Trail)

The trail starts from the back of the parking lot and follows blue blazes up alongside Bully Brook. The Brook has two cascades about 0.5 mile into the trail. There are nice views to the north as the route ascends to the Long Trail. At the junction with the Long Trail, head south (right) for about 0.3 mile. Rock cairns and a sign mark the trail that descends 0.2 mile to the cliffs, with their splendid views to the south, west, north, and overlooking the ice beds. Here you will find interesting rock formations and multiple spots to sit and enjoy lunch. This trail may be closed at times because of Peregrine Falcon nesting.

Total time 2 hours, 2.6 miles, Elevation gain: 1,150'
Approach: From Wallingford (US 7) at the junction with VT 140, head left 2.1 miles. Bear right onto Sugar Road. Signs will direct you to the Forest Service picnic area.

White Rocks Cliffs   Jared Gange

8 Mount Ascutney Area

The isolated shape of Mount Ascutney (3,150') is one of Vermont's best-known landmarks. Located in the town of Windsor, near the Connecticut River, Ascutney is unchallenged by other peaks and is clearly visible for many miles throughout New Hampshire and Vermont. Although Ascutney is lower than many Vermont summits, its relative isolation and solid vertical rise contribute to make this one of the best mountain views in Vermont. In geologic terms, Mount Ascutney is a classic monadnock. Formerly the site of extensive granite quarrying and logging, Ascutney is today a recreation destination. In addition to Mount Ascutney Ski Area and Mount Ascutney State Park, there are four hiking trails to the top, a hang glider launch area and a paved toll road to the 2,750' level.

60 Ascutney via Weathersfield Trail

The blue-blazed Weathersfield Trail passes two cascades and numerous viewpoints on its varied route to the top. In particular, 84-foot-high **Crystal Cascade** (at 1.2 miles) is noteworthy, as it reveals Ascutney's geologic origins. **Gus' Lookout** (2,700'), at 2.3 miles, is open to the south, and at 2.6 miles, a short spur trail leads to **West Peak** with its excellent views. Take the left fork just before the summit to reach the observation tower and its 360-degree vista. Descend by the same route. Mount Ascutney's mid-state location provides a perfect spot to view Vermont's Green Mountains, as well as the mountains of New Hampshire.

4 hours and 5.8 miles round trip. Elevation gain: 2,060'
Approach: Drive 3.3 miles west on Route 131 from the Ascutney exit on I-91, turn right on to Cascade Falls Rd., and follow signs to the trailhead parking.

Mount Ascutney and the Connecticut RIver   Jared Gange

61 Mount Ascutney via Brownsville Trail

An excellent and varied hike, the Brownsville Trail starts out steeply, then follows a moderately graded road to an old granite quarry. After negotiating some rougher terrain, the trail settles into a steady climb passing various viewpoints and joins with the **Windsor Trail** before reaching the summit observation tower. From a clearing 0.2 mile before the tower, a short spur leads right to **Brownsville Rock** with its bird's-eye view of the surrounding area. Descend by the same route or by the Windsor Trail.

4.5 hours and 6.4 miles round trip. Gain: 2,400'

Approach: From the village of Windsor, drive 4.6 miles west on Route 44 and park in the small trailhead parking lot on the south side of the highway.

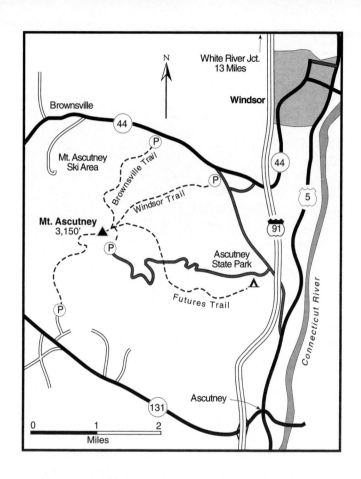

The ***Mount Ascutney Guide*** gives a history of the mountain and detailed trail information with two maps. The Ascutney Trails Association of Windsor, Vermont, publishes it.

62 Mount Ascutney via Windsor Trail

Originally a road, this popular trail is the most direct route to the top. From Route 44A, the trail starts out in a field but soon enters the woods and climbs more steeply. On this long-used route (white blazes), you pass the sites of old cabins and various dramatic episodes of yesteryear. At about 2.5 miles, the stone hut clearing is reached (take the short detour right to spectacular **Brownsville Rock**), and the summit tower is just beyond. Descend by the same trail or by Brownsville Trail. The road distance between the two trailheads is 1.2 miles.

4.5 hours and 5.4 miles round trip. Gain: 2,520'

Approach: From Windsor, drive about 3.5 miles west on Route 44 to Route 44A. Then turn left on to Route 44A for a short distance to the trail parking lot on your right.

63 Okemo Mountain 3,343' (Ludlow)

From the tower on Okemo's summit, the hiker is rewarded by a 360-degree view of mountains near and far. Completed in 1993 by Vermont's Youth Conservation Corps, the **Healdville Trail** ascends the north side of the mountain over mixed terrain. The first third climbs moderately, followed by an easier section before the final steeper climb to the top. Stay right at the junction near the top. Descend by the same trail.

4 hours and 5.8 miles round trip. Elevation gain: 1,940'

Approach: From Ludlow, drive north on Route 100 to Route 103. Continue 3 miles on Route 103 to Station Road, turn left, and proceed 0.8 mile to the trailhead parking area.

64 Mount Tom 1,250' (Woodstock)

A pleasant, very gently graded path, complete with occasional benches, leads to the top of Woodstock's local mountain. It is the sort of path you would expect to find on a mountainside in Europe. Pick up the trail at the rear of **Faulkner Park**, and after many switchbacks crest a knoll just below the summit. Continue a short ways on a steeper and rougher path to the actual top of Mt. Tom, where there are excellent views of Woodstock and the surrounding area.

2 hours and 3 miles round trip. Elevation gain: 550'

Approach: Drive or walk to Faulkner Park, on Mountain Avenue, across the covered bridge in Woodstock.

65 Quechee Gorge

Quechee Gorge is a 165-foot deep gorge of the Ottauquechee River. The vantage point from the Route 4 bridge provides an impressive view of what locals affectionately refer to as Vermont's "Little Grand Canyon". Hiking down into the gorge will give you interesting perspectives on this dramatic bit of landscape, and, on a hot summer day, the opportunity to swim (use caution). The Quechee Gorge Trail begins to the west of the parking area and, after bearing left, runs down to the water. People swim at their own risk where the gorge's grade slackens, after the channel divides. Hike back up the way you came.

1 hour and 1 mile round trip. Elevation gain: 200'

Approach: From I-89, exit 2, follow US Route 4 west towards Woodstock. The gorge is 6 miles east of Woodstock and 5 miles west of I-89. When approaching from the east, park on the right side of the road, at the gift shops just before the bridge.

The east side of Cardigan, the Holt Trail   Jared Gange

Mount Cardigan 3,121' (N.H.)

Although a low mountain, Cardigan's bare, rocky summit gives the feel of a higher peak. It is one of the classic mountains of New Hampshire and very popular with kids. From the picnic area, follow the **West Ridge Trail**. It ascends at an easy angle, meeting several other trails along the way. The upper portion runs across bare ledges; you soon reach the wide-open summit area with its panoramic views. The firetower is manned, and it is often possible to visit with the ranger and learn about the mountain and its history. Descend by the same route. A variation is to take the **Clark Trail** (sign) off the summit. At the **South Ridge Trail**, turn right and take it back down to the car.

2 hours and 3 miles round trip. Elevation gain: 1,220'
Approach: From Canaan (take exit 17 off I-89 to Enfield) on Route 4, continue 0.5 mile north on Route 118. Turn right, follow signs, and continue through Orange to Cardigan State Park and the trailhead.

Manchester and Stratton Mountain

Manchester lies in the narrow valley formed by the Taconic Range to the west and the Green Mountains to the east. In this area most of the mountain hiking is linked to the Long Trail, with the Taconics seeing less activity. However, impressive Mount Equinox, which looms directly over Manchester to the west, is perhaps the area's best climb, while a paved road to the top provides easy access to the summit trails.

66 Mt. Equinox 3,825'

Mt. Equinox rises almost 3,000' above Manchester and is arguably the dominant mountain of the area, Stratton included. The **Burr and Burton Trail** ascends the mountain from the east, from Manchester Village, just south of Manchester Center. From the parking area, the blue-blazed trail first follows a woods road but soon branches right and begins its steady climb. After about 2 miles, the trail is less steep, and at 2.7 miles, you reach the intersection with the **Yellow Trail** and **Red Trail**. The Yellow Trail heads north (right) for 0.5 mile over relatively easy terrain to **Lookout Rock**, where there are excellent views of the surrounding mountains and the valley below. From here, take **Lookout Rock Trail** on to the summit and the Skyline Inn (upper end of the Equinox Skyline Drive). To descend, take Lookout Rock Trail for 0.1 mile then turn right on the Burr and Burton Trail and take it back down.

5–6 hours and 5.8 miles round trip. Gain: 2,880'
Approach: From Manchester Ctr., take Route 7A south for a mile. Turn right on Seminary Street. Park behind the Burr and Burton School. The trail starts from the upper lot.

A hiker locates peaks from a open summit   Jared Gange

67 Prospect Rock 2,179'

A favorite short hike, Prospect Rock offers great views of Manchester, Mount Equinox, and to the north, Dorset Peak. From the gate at the end of the public road, start up the steep and rocky roadway (Old Rootville Road) and continue for about 1.5 miles to the Long Trail. The spur trail to Prospect Rock is about 120' farther south on the Long Trail, on your right. Return by the way you came.

2.5 hours and 3 miles round trip. Elevation gain: 1,000'

Approach: Drive east from Manchester Center (on Routes 11/30), turning right on East Manchester Road then left on Rootville Road. Limited parking at the end of the road.

68 Stratton Mountain 3,936'

The conventional hiking route up Stratton is from the south, via the **Long Trail**, although climbing the mountain from the ski area (north side) also is recommended. The fire tower on the top of Stratton's South Peak, 0.8 mile south of the gondola terminal, provides a panoramic view extending to five states. From the parking area on Kelley Stand Road, follow the LT north for 3.3 miles to the tower. From the summit, the LT descends (left) 2.6 miles to secluded, but popular, **Stratton Pond**, an important stopover with LT/AT thru-hikers. There are several shelters here, and during hiking season, GMC caretakers are in residence. Return to the car via the gradually descending 4-mile **Stratton Pond Trail** (blue blazes), which ends on Kelley Stand Road, a mile west of your starting point.

7-8 hours and 11 miles round trip. Gain: 1,910'

Approach: From Arlington, drive east, or from the village of Stratton, drive west on the Arlington–West Wardsboro Road (Kelley Stand Road) to the Long Trail parking area.

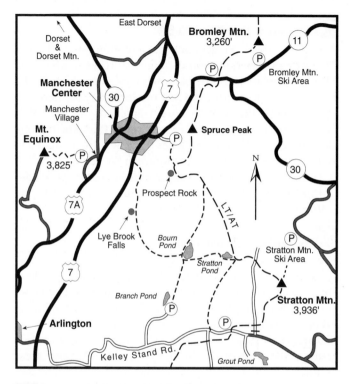

69 Stratton Mountain via ski trails

From the base of the ski area, bear right through the little ski village to the base of the gondola. The hike up the open ski trails runs to the north summit (ca. 3,885') and will take about an hour to an hour and a half. It is 0.7 mile (about 20 minutes) over to the higher south summit with its observation tower. Note that the lift runs during the summer season, so it is possible to ride up or down — or both!

70 Spruce Peak 2,040'

A popular hike over generally easy terrain, this trail gains only 240' in elevation from the highway. Head south on the LT/AT. There are a couple of viewpoints along the way, and from the short spur trail (right) on Spruce Peak, there is a good view to the west of Mount Equinox and the valley below. Return by the same route. **Spruce Peak Shelter**, one of the finest cabins on the LT, lies 0.5 mile farther south and is at a somewhat higher elevation than Spruce Peak.

2.5 hours and 4.5 miles round trip. Elevation gain: 240'
Approach: From Manchester Ctr., drive east 5 miles on Routes 11/30 to the Long Trail highway crossing.

71 Bromley Mountain 3,260'

Hike north on the Long Trail/Appalachian Trail over generally moderate terrain to reach the top of Bromley, where there is a cafeteria and a good observation deck. The views south to Stratton Ski Area and of the other nearby mountains are excellent. Descend by the same route, or, as an alternative to trail walking, hike down the steep, grassy ski trails to the base of the Bromley ski area. (Arrange a car shuttle.)

4 hours and 5.6 miles round trip. Elevation gain: 1,460'
Approach: From Manchester Center, drive east on Routes 11 and 30 for 5 miles to the large parking area on the left, which is where the Long Trail crosses the highway.

Similar to Stratton Mountain, the ski runs at Bromley offer a great route up the mountain. As you climb the open, grassy slopes, the views just get better and better. From the base of the ski area, on Route 11, just east of the junction of Routes 11 and 30, follow lifts and ski trails to the top.

Negotiating a steep & rough section   Lars Gange

72 Lye Brook Falls

Lye Brook Falls is one of the highest waterfalls/cascades in Vermont. From the parking area, take the Lye Brook Trail south (marked with blue blazes) for about 2 miles until it crosses an old railroad bed. Here, head right on the railroad bed for 0.3 mile to the falls. Return by the same route.

2.5 hours and 4 miles round trip. Elevation gain: 1,000'
Approach: From Route 11/30, east of Manchester Center, turn right onto Richville Road, then left on East Manchester Road. After the underpass, head right on Glen Road; at the fork, bear right for another 0.5 of a mile to the trailhead parking at the end of the road.

73 Griffith Lake and Baker Peak 2,850'

Although well below treeline, Baker has a rocky, partially exposed summit with a sweeping westerly view from Equinox in the south to Dorset Peak and many miles to the north. Take the **Lake Trail** (moderately steep) reaching **Baker Peak Trail** at 2 miles, after crossing McGinn Brook. After a mile of mostly easy walking (a few steep parts), you reach the **Long Trail**. Head left (north) on the LT for 0.1 mile to the top. Descend either by the same route or head south on the LT (easy terrain) for 1.9 miles to lovely **Griffith Lake**. From the lake, backtrack on the LT to the Lake Trail and the car.

Loop: 5–6 hours, 9 miles round trip. Gain: 2,350'

Approach: From Manchester, drive north on Route 7, 2.4 miles past Emerald Lake to Town Highway 5. Turn right and park on the left after 0.5 mile.

74 Little Rock Pond 1,850'

An easy hike takes you to a pretty pond nestled in a forested mountain setting. The well-used shelters and platforms in the vicinity attest to the area's popularity! Follow the LT (AT, too) north over easy terrain for 2 miles to reach the pond. A variation (longer) to the overlook on Green Mtn. (2,509') gives you the much-photographed view of the pond below. It is worth the extra effort: Continue past the southern end of the pond to **Green Mountain Trail**, then head left about 30 minutes. Return the same route or continue on this trail back to Mount Tabor Road. The longer variations total 6 or 7.5 miles respectively.

2 hours, 4-5 miles round trip. Elevation gain: 350'

Approach: From Manchester Ctr., take Rt. 7 north to Danby. Turn right on FS #10 (Mt. Tabor Road) and continue to the Appalachian Trail/Long Trail crossing.

Hiker negotiating a wet slab

Jared Gange

Rime ice   Jared Gange

75 Mount Antone 2,620'

Great views of the Dorset area await you at the top of
Antone. The unblazed trail begins on Old Towne Road and
continues past a fork (stay right) and a couple of intersections. Expect pleasant views of the Adirondacks along this
road. At a well-marked junction, the Mount Antone road
heads off to the right. Follow this road south — past an
overnight shelter — and climb steeply up to the ridge top.
Stay on the Mount Antone road as it descends, intersects
with several roads, and finally ascends to the summit. From
the summit a spur trail bends downward, offering great
views of the nearby Adirondacks in New York.

3.5 hours, 5 miles round trip. Elevation gain: 890'
Approach: From the junction of VT 315 and VT 30 in East
Rupert drive west on VT 315 for 2.4 miles to the Merck
Forest sign on the left. Turn left on to the dirt road and
continue to a gate and a 10-car parking area at 2.9 miles.

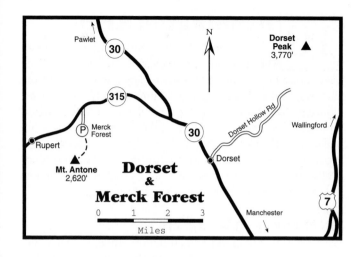

Dorset Peak 3,770'

The trail up this attractive, steep-sided (but viewless) peak is not maintained; however, it is climbed regularly. Dorset Peak is one of New England's 100 highest peaks and is a requirement for those on that particular quest. Similar in appearance to Equinox, it is very prominent from Route 7 when approaching from the north. The first mile of the route is negotiable with a 4-wheel drive vehicle. From a logging clearing, the trail ascends steeply past a hunting camp and continues to the saddle west of the summit before contouring around to the north. This trip is recommended only for hikers who are very experienced with route finding.

5 hours and 7 miles round trip. Elevation gain: 2,300'

Approach: From Dorset (west of Manchester Center), follow Dorset Hollow Rd., then Tower Rd. to the end of the valley, about 4 miles from Dorset. The trailhead is unmarked.

10 Bennington Area

Bennington is in the southwestern corner of the state, only 11 miles from Massachusetts. The main ridge of the Green Mountains lies a few miles to the east, while the Taconic Range is immediately to the west along the New York border. We describe several Bennington favorites as well as three hikes approached from Massachusetts. Two of them, Mount Greylock (3,491'), and Pine Cobble are *in* Massachusetts. The Greylock-Williamstown area has a well-developed trail network and its proximity to Bennington makes it worth visiting.

76 Harmon Hill 2,320'

Harmon Hill is a popular Bennington hike, giving good, close views of the town and the nearby Taconic mountains. The Forest Service keeps the summit area clear of brush by annual, controlled burns. From the parking on Route 9, head south on the **Long Trail**, at times quite steeply, reaching the top of Harmon Hill at about 1.7 miles. The steep sections of the trail use rock and log steps. Return by the same route.

2.5 hours and 3.4 miles round trip. Gain: 1,265'

Approach: From Bennington, drive east on Route 9 for 5 miles to the Long Trail crossing and the trailhead parking.

77 Bald Mountain 2,857'

The 7-mile **Bald Mtn. Trail** starts on North Branch Street in Bennington and traverses Bald Mountain, ending in Woodford Hollow, on the east side of the mountain. The shorter option is from the Woodford side. From your car, follow the blue-blazed trail first along old road beds, then up through a series of switchbacks, reaching the **West Ridge Trail** at 2.5 miles. Head right (north) for 0.1 mile to reach the top. Various points near the summit offer good views of Bennington and the nearby mountains. Return by the same route. The West Ridge Trail continues north, then east, for 7.6 miles to meet the Long Trail near Goddard Shelter on Glastenbury Mountain. See the loop hike described below.

4 hours and 5.2 miles round trip. Elevation gain: 1,600'
Approach: From Bennington, drive east 4 miles on Route 9 to the Woodford church. Head left on a gravel road for 0.8 mile to the trailhead, at a concrete water tank.

Stone stairway in a birch forest   J. Gange

78 Glastenbury Mountain 3,747'

From Route 9, hike north on the Long Trail (and AT), most of the time in dense woods, passing two outlooks along the way. Plan to overnight at **Goddard Shelter** (lean-to with room for 10 people), 9.8 miles from the car. The summit and observation tower are 0.3 mile beyond the shelter. The view is one of a huge forest expanse, with few signs of man's intrusion upon nature. Return the next day by the same route, or, more interestingly, by the **West Ridge Trail** over **Bald Mountain** and down to Woodford (see above). The Bald Mountain variation takes a little longer.

12–13 hours (2 days), 20-mile loop, Gain: 2,400'

Approach: From Bennington, drive 5 miles east on Route 9 to the trailhead parking area where the Long Trail crosses the highway.

79 The Dome 2,748'

From the trailhead, follow the **Dome Trail** for 2.9 miles to the summit of Dome. At 1.5 miles, the **Agawon Trail** comes in from the right. The final half mile of the trail is rocky and interesting, and from the exposed rocks on the summit, there are good views of Mount Greylock, the Berkshires, the Taconics, and southern Vermont. The Dome Trail, blazed in orange, is maintained by Williams Outing Club at Williams College . The Dome is in Vermont, but the approach is from Massachusetts.

3.5 hours and 5.8 miles round trip. Elevation gain: 1,700'

Approach: From Route 7, 1.5 miles south of the Vt.-Mass. border, turn left (east) on Sand Springs Road. At White Oaks Road, turn left; park after 1.5 miles, 0.3 mile back inside Vermont. See the map on the next page.

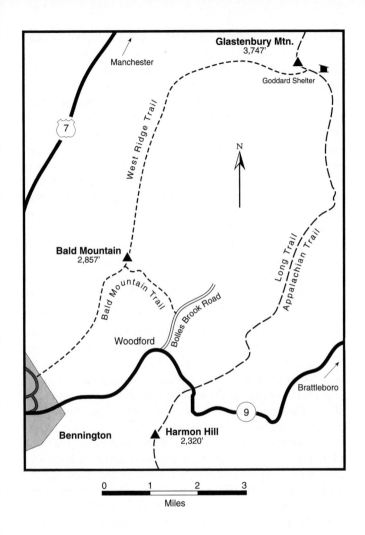

Glastenbury Mtn.
3,747'

Goddard Shelter

Manchester

West Ridge Trail

7

N

Bald Mountain
2,857'

Bald Mountain Trail

Bolles Brook Road

Long Trail

Appalachian Trail

Woodford

Bennington

Harmon Hill
2,320'

9

Brattleboro

| 0 | 1 | 2 | 3 |
Miles

Mount Greylock 3,491' (Massachusetts)

The highest mountain in the state, Greylock is an impressive sight. It is graced with many hiking trails, including the Appalachian Trail. Popular **Bascom Lodge**, on the top, is an important milestone for AT thru-hikers. The **Hopper Trail**, perhaps the classic route, climbs steeply up the north flank of the Hopper, a huge ravine on the west side. From the parking area, walk first along easy terrain before bearing right and climbing, reaching Sperry Rd. after about an hour (2 miles). The route then merges with Deer Hill Trail, passing Rockwell Rd. twice before meeting the AT (white blazes). Follow this to the summit. Return by the same route.

5 hours and 8.2 miles round trip. Elevation gain: 2,340'
Approach: From Williamstown (south of Bennington), drive east on Rt. 2 for a short distance before turning right onto Water St. Continue south for 2.6 miles then turn left on Hopper Road; follow this 2.7 miles to the parking area.

Since Williamstown is close to Bennington — about 30 minutes — and since it has so much to offer the hiker, it is hard to resist mentioning a few more hikes while we are in the area. **Mount Greylock**, Massachusetts' highest, has an extensive trail network, and one of its classic routes is discussed above. **Pine Cobble** (1,894') is a shorter hike and immensely popular with the college students. Figure on about two to two and a half hours round trip from the campus. The blue-blazed trail climbs 1,200' to reach the quartzite summit outcrop with its spectacular views across to Greylock and the Taconic Range; the "Purple Valley" spreads out below. From the campus, head north on Cole Avenue from Main Street, cross the river, and bear slightly to the right and uphill on a private road, which soon transitions to the trail. From the top of Pine Cobble it is possible to pick up the AT and con-

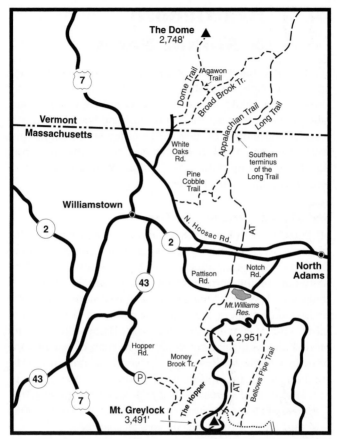

tinue north to Vermont. In Williamstown, the **Williams Outing Club** (W.O.C.) at Williams College maintains the trails in the Williamstown area and produces an excellent guide book: the *W. O. C. Trail Guide and Map*, which describes over 30 trails, including the Dome, Pine Cobble, and Mount Greylock.

11 Brattleboro & Mount Snow

We give five hikes in the southeastern corner of the state and two in New Hampshire. Mount Olga, Mount Snow, and Haystack Mountain are near Wilmington, while Bald Mountain enjoys relative isolation in Townshend State Park, northwest of Brattleboro, off Route 30. Putney Mountain lies just west of Putney. Mt. Wantastiquet, just across the river from Brattleboro, along with fabled Mount Monadnock, east of Keene, complete the chapter.

80 Mount Snow 3,556'

Mt. Snow is the home of a large alpine ski area, which in the summer is a major mountain biking center. Generally not as steep as many other alpine areas, Mount Snow is excellent mountain biking terrain. Climb the mountain by the ski trails, which offer hiking on open, grassy slopes. From the rocky summit, there are extensive views of southern Vermont and Massachusetts, and New Hampshire's Mount Monadnock is picked out easily. There is an excellent view of nearby Somerset Reservoir. The gondola runs during the summer, giving the option of riding up and walking down.

2.5 hours and 3 miles round trip. Elevation gain: 1,500'
Approach: From Wilmington, drive north on Route 100 to Mount Snow. Park at the ski area base lodge.

The **Deerfield Trail** connects the top of Mt. Snow with the top of Haystack Ski Area. Primarily a cross country ski and snowmobile trail, this 3-mile trail segment is negotiable in summer but is quite rough and therefore something for more experienced and self-sufficient hikers.

A young skier crosses a beaver pond Jared Gange

81 Haystack Mountain 3,420'

Haystack Mountain is one of the more popular and interesting mountain hikes in southeastern Vermont. It is a satellite of Mount Snow, but for hikers Haystack has more significance. From the summit, there is a good view of **Haystack Pond** about 500' below, as shown above. Many of the mountains of southern Vermont can be seen, and Mount Greylock in western Massachusetts, is also visible. Once the trailhead is located, the blue-blazed trail is easy to follow. Carefully note trail intersections on the way up for your return trip.

3 hours and 4.8 miles. Elevation gain: 1,030'

Approach: From Wilmington, drive west on Rt. 9 for 1.1 miles and turn right on Haystack Rd. Continue on Haystack, staying right, to Chimney Hill Rd. at about 1.2 miles. Turn left here, then right on Binney Brook Rd. At 2.6 miles from Rt. 9, reach the trailhead on the right.

Maps: USGS *Mt. Snow, Townshend* and *Keene.*

82 Mount Olga 2,415'

From the fire tower on Mount Olga's wooded summit there are sweeping views. The loop trail from **Molly Stark State Park** is blue-blazed and easy to follow. Mount Olga also can be climbed directly from Route 9, up the open ski trails (good views) of Hogback Ski Area. For those with less time, this alternative is shorter and offers less climbing.

Loop: 1.5 hours and 1.6 miles. Elevation gain: 500'

Approach: Mount Olga is located in Molly Stark State Park, 3.4 miles east of Wilmington, just south of Route 9. It is about 14 miles west of Brattleboro.

Map: A free hiker's map is available at the campground

83 Bald Mountain 1,680'

This modest mountain offers a good hike with a moderate climb. There are views of Bromley, Stratton, and the West River Valley from the summit. The trail starts from the campground, crossing and recrossing a brook before reaching the top after about 1.4 miles. The standard loop is done by descending the mountain via the steeper north side trail, which returns to the campground.

Loop: 2.5 hours and 2.8 miles. Elevation gain: 1,100'

Approach: From Townshend (20 miles from Brattleboro), drive west on Rt. 30. Cross the river at Townshend Dam and turn left back along the river (passing Vermont's longest single span covered bridge) to Townshend State Park.

Map: A free hiker's map is available at the campground.

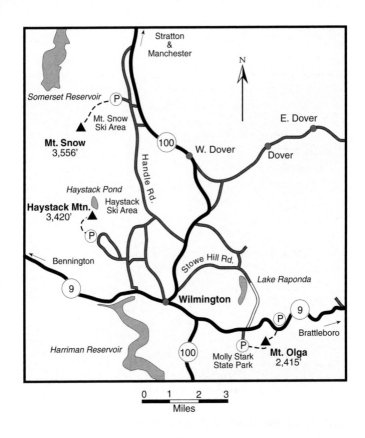

Maps: DeLorme's Vermont Atlas and Gazetteer, pages 21-23.

Hikers nearing the summit of Mt. Monadnock   J. Gange

84 Fort Dummer State Park

A self-guided mile-long loop (Sunrise Trail) provides access to two lookouts where there are views of the Connecticut River and the nearby mountains, including Mt. Monadnock. Pick up a trail map at the park office.

45 minutes, 1 mile round trip

Approach: From US 5, just south of Brattleboro, take Fairgrounds Rd. then right on South Main to the end.

Mt. Wantastiquet 1,351' (New Hampshire)

Although not in Vermont, Mount Wantastiquet is Brattleboro's local hike. In fact, it is easy to walk right from downtown to the top. From the parking area (see the approach directions below), follow the (gated) road to the top where there are good views of the area.

1.5 hours and 1.4 miles round trip. Gain: 1,200'

Approach: From Brattleboro, cross the Connecticut River into New Hampshire and take the left *immediately* after the bridge. Park at the gate after about a quarter of a mile.

Mt. Monadnock 3,165' (New Hampshire)

Mount Monadnock is one of the great classic hikes of New England, and its proximity to Brattleboro makes it an important "local" hike. Consult a New Hampshire hiking guide (e.g. *Hiker's Guide to the Mountains of New Hampshire*) for more information on Monadnock. The route we have chosen, the **Marlboro Trail**, starts out with easy grades but steepens, alternating between forest pockets and open rock ledges. About a half mile from the top, the summit area comes into view, and the **Dublin Trail** enters from the left. The upper part of Monadnock is a fantastic expanse of bare rock — the result of fires over a hundred years ago — and in good weather is a great place to hang out. Descend by the same route, carefully noting trail intersections. The Marlboro Trail receives much less traffic than the trails from Monadnock State Park.

3¼ hours and 4.4 miles. Elevation gain: 1,865'

Approach: 35 miles from Brattleboro, and well inside New Hampshire, Monadnock draws hikers from southern Vermont. From NH 124, 5 miles east of Marlboro, head left 0.7 miles on Shaker Farm Rd. to the trailhead.

12 | Groton State Forest

This popular recreation area is located east of Montpelier. It is heavily forested, but the numerous lakes and some interesting rock outcrops make it an area worth exploring. The state park (within the state forest) has several campgrounds and a network of hiking trails as well as other recreation possibilities. There is a day usage fee, but a free trail guide and map is available at the park entrance.

Approach: From Barre, take Route 302 east to Route 232, turn left, and drive past Lake Groton to Groton State Park.

85 Owl's Head 1,958'

This is a popular hike with great views of Lake Groton and beautiful Kettle Pond. On the top, trails on smooth granite bedrock radiate in all directions through spruces and blueberry bushes. The hiking trail begins off the road to **Osmore Pond**, and after avoiding a swampy area, climbs up to a parking area. It is then a steep 0.1 mile to the top.

1.5 hours and 3 miles round trip. Elevation gain: 230'
Approach: From New Discovery Campground B, follow signs to the trail. *Note:* The easy way to "hike" Owl's Head is to drive up the gravel road, which goes to within 0.1 mile of the actual summit.

86 Big Deer Mountain 1,992'

Big Deer is similar to Owl's Head but offers a slightly higher and less-visited summit with excellent views of nearby lakes and surrounding mountains. The first mile of the **Big Deer Mountain Trail** is quite easy, with the last half mile climbing steeply up to the summit area. The trail has blue blazes.

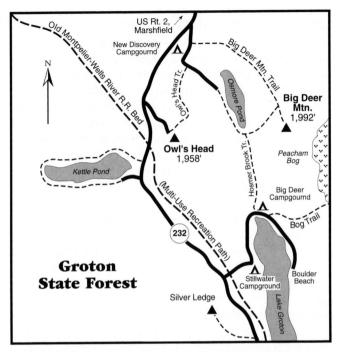

2 hours and 3.4 miles round trip. Elevation gain: 250'
Approach: Drive through the park entrance to where Campground B begins and turn left on the road to **Peacham Pond** for 0.3 mile. The trailhead is on the right with limited parking.
Maps: *USGS Marshfield, Knox Mountain and*
Montpelier (1:100 000) and DeLorme Atlas, page 41

87 Spruce Mountain 3,037'

Located at the western edge of Groton State Forest, only the summit of Spruce is in the Forest, and the mountain is some distance away from Lake Groton. From the gate, follow the woods road to the right, staying on it for about a mile as it swings to the south side of the mountain. At 1.5 miles, the trail begins a more or less steady climb to the top, at times passing across exposed granite. From the tower on the summit, there are excellent views in all directions. Descend by the same route. Nearby **Signal Mountain**, at 3,348', is the highest mountain in this range, but there is no hiking trail to the summit.

3 hours, 4.4 miles round trip. Elevation gain: 1,340'
Approach: From Plainfield, drive south on East Hill Road for 4.3 miles and turn left on Spruce Mtn. Rd. Turn left at the next junction and continue uphill to the gate and parking.

88 Kettle Pond Trail

This pleasant hike skirts the shoreline of a beautiful, secluded pond. It takes an hour or two and is a good hike for families. The trail is somewhat rocky and wet at the far end of the pond. Starting from the highway, walk around the pond in a clockwise fashion, ending at the Kettle Pond Group Camping Area just south of where you began the hike.

1-2 hours, 3-mile loop. Elevation gain: negligible
Approach: Parking on the west side of the road, about a mile south of the side road up Owl's Head.

View of Owl's Head in Groton State Forest   Vt. Dept. of FPR

Montpelier-Wells River Rail Trail

Inside Groton State Forest, the old roadbed of the now defunct Montpelier-Wells River Railroad offers about 7 miles of easy, evenly graded roadway that is great for biking, hiking, cross country skiing, and snowmobiling.

The area has a fascinating history. In 1873, growing industry, especially logging, led to the establishment of the railroad, which served the area until its closure in the mid-1950s. In its heyday, the Montpelier-Wells River Railroad carried myriad goods, including farm products, granite, and summer tourists. This rail line was linked to Boston and Maine, so summer vacationers could be let off in what is now Groton State Forest and set up camp and explore the area's lakes and hills.

13 Northeast Kingdom

The cool deep waters of Lake Willoughby (a land-locked fjord) are a mecca for fishermen, while the cliffs of Mount Pisgah offer some of the best ice climbing in the Northeast. Although the summits are wooded and well below the treeline, the hikes in this region offer some of the most spectacular views in Vermont. Lake Willoughby is about 22 miles north of St. Johnsbury. Nearby Burke Mountain and remote Mount Monadnock are also interesting.

89 Mount Pisgah 2,751'

Mount Pisgah is one of Vermont's more dramatic mountains, and the view of **Lake Willoughby** from the top of the 1,000' cliffs will not disappoint you. The popular **South Trail** leaves the highway and crosses a pond area on bridges. The trail then ascends very steeply, before passing perch-like **Pulpit Rock**, with its aerial view of the south end of the lake. The main trail is safe enough, but the wooded mountainside is extremely steep—use caution! After another sustained climb, the gradient eases before reaching a rock slab with sweeping views to the south. The wooded summit is just beyond, at 1.7 miles, where a spur trail leads right to an interesting view of Bald Mtn. From the top, descend a short way to reach the famous viewpoints (left) atop Pisgah's cliffs. They are larger and safer than Pulpit Rock. Descend the way you came up.

2.5 hours, 3.5 miles. Elevation gain: 1,450'

Approach: From Lyndonville, take Rt. 114 to West Burke then Rt. 5A for 6 miles to a parking area (left) just south of Lake Willoughby. The South Trail begins across the highway.

Mount Pisgah from the south   Jared Gange

90 Mount Pisgah from the north

The popular 2.2-mile **North Trail** also starts from Route 5A, at a point 3 miles north of South Trail's trailhead. The path climbs on an old woods road, first at a moderate pitch then more steeply, until it reaches the junction with the trail to Long Pond. From here, the trail climbs less steeply and passes side trails (right) to North Lookout and West Lookout. The upper lookout offers the more impressive view of Lake Willoughby, 1,400' below. The North and South Trails meet at the wooded summit. Return by the same route.

2.5 hours, 3.5 miles. Elevation gain: 1,050'

Approach: From Lyndonville, take Rt. 114 to West Burke then Rt. 5A for 9 miles to roadside parking on the right side of the highway.

91 Mount Hor 2,648'

Mount Hor is directly across Lake Willoughby from Mount Pisgah, and its main attraction is the spectacular view of the lake and Pisgah's cliffs. The blue-blazed trail does not actually go to the top of Mt. Hor but does lead to several viewpoints. After 0.7 mile, the trail forks. Take the right fork another 0.7 mile to **East Lookout**, where there is a superb view of Mount Pisgah, and to **North Lookout**, with impressive views of the lake and north into Canada. The left fork climbs 0.3 mile to **Summit Lookout**, with good views to the west.

2 hours and 2.8 miles round trip. Elevation gain: 700'
Approach: Turn left (west) off Route 5A, about 6 miles north of West Burke and drive up a gravel road (the CCC Road) for 1.8 miles to a parking area on the right.

92 Wheeler Mountain 2,371'

This popular, short hike has the feel of a rock climb as you clamber up and across smooth granite slabs. After a short distance, the trail divides into the **Red Trail** (shorter, steeper) and the **White Trail**. They merge just below the top. Most hikers will enjoy the steeper ascent, followed by the slightly longer White Trail on the descent. After reaching the summit ledges, continue a few minutes to spectacular **Eagle Cliff** where there are better views towards Lake Willoughby and of the surrounding area. The clean granite slabs make this hike unusual for Vermont. A somewhat similar but longer hike is Maple Ridge on Mt. Mansfield.

2 hours and 2 miles round trip. Elevation gain: 700'
Approach: From Route 5, 8.3 miles north of West Burke, turn right on to Wheeler Pond Road, and drive for 2 miles to a small signed parking area on the left.

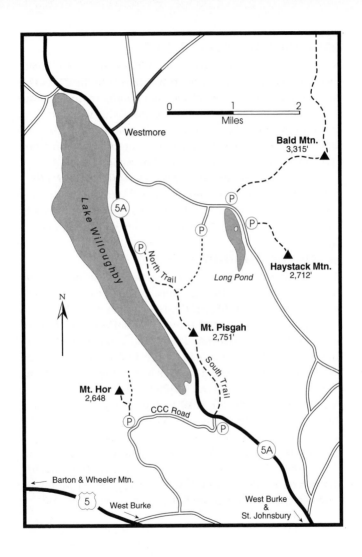

93 Bald Mountain 3,315'

With its summit tower, and as the highest mountain in the Lake Willoughby area, Bald Mtn. offers the best general views in the region. There are two routes to the summit (note map).The Long Pond route starts about 100 yards east of the pond access. Using various old woods roads, the trail ascends generally moderately to the summit with only limited views along the way. Descend by same trail.

3 hours and 4 miles round trip. Elevation gain: 1,450'

Approach: From Westmore (Lake Willoughby), drive 2 miles east on Long Pond Road to Long Pond and park at the lake access parking or just beyond, at the trailhead.

94 Burke Mountain 3,267'

Home of Burke Mountain Ski Area, Burke also offers good hiking and mountain biking.There is a road to the top (hiking is allowed, car toll), but the best hiking route begins as a small road to the right of the ski area parking lot.After 0.8 mile, take the red-blazed trail (left) and climb about 800' to the fire road. Here, at a lean-to, the trail divides, with the blue-blazed route taking a steeper line to the summit ridge. The two trails rejoin about 50 feet below the top of West Peak. Follow the **Profile Trail** to the summit tower, where there are excellent views of Mount Pisgah and nearby mountains. Descend by same route or by ski trails.

2.5 hours and 3.5 miles round trip. Gain: 1,270'

Approach: From East Burke (just north of Lyndonville), continue 1 mile on Mountain Road to the Burke Mountain Sherburne Lodge parking lots.

95 Mount Monadnock 3,140'

Vermont's Mount Monadnock, in the extreme northeastern corner of the state, is a local landmark, rising over 2,000' above the Connecticut River. Although it is a fine hike, on a good trail, Monadnock is almost unknown to hikers outside the area. From the bridge, walk south along the highway about 100' and turn right on to a private road. This soon turns into a trail, and climbing steeply, crosses a stream (45 minutes) and continues to climb steeply before slackening and reaching the summit after about 2 hours. The trail is viewless until the top. Climb the tower (needs repair) to get above the trees for spectacular views of the North Country, into Canada, and of New Hampshire's Mt. Washington and the Presidential Range. Analogous to Mt. Ascutney, both are monadnocks located on the west bank of the Connecticut River. Mt. Monadnock is only 10 feet lower than its southern cousin.

3.5 hours and 5 miles round trip. Elevation gain: 2,100'
Approach: Across the river from Colebrook, NH, Mount Monadnock is on Route 102, about 30 miles east of Island Pond. Park just south of the Route 26 bridge on Rt. 102.

14 The Northern Frontier

The mountains traversed by the Long Trail from Route 15 north to Canada are sometimes referred to as the Northern Frontier. Although less visited than the terrain to the south, there is fine hiking in this wilder, more remote part of the state. A good deal of the Long Trail runs across private land, and the Green Mountain Club is working with landowners in the area to secure permanent protection for the Long Trail corridor. From the summit of Belvidere Mountain, it is only 27 miles to the Canadian border.

96 Belvidere Mountain 3,360'

A fine, distinct mountain in an isolated setting, Belvidere offers a very worthwhile hike. On a windy day, the sensation from the 70' fire tower is like flying! The route follows the **Long Trail** north from Rt. 118 and offers pleasant walking on an interesting and varied trail. Although here in the more northern part of the state, the forest is lower and sparser than farther south, views still are limited until the top is reached. At Belvidere Saddle (3,200'), leave the Long Trail (right) and take the Forester's Trail the final 0.2 mile to the top. (Note that the Forester's Trail also descends from the saddle northeast to the asbestos mine access road, 4.5 miles north of Route 118.) From the top, it seems the whole of northern Vermont is on display. Return the way you came.

4 hours and 5.6 miles round trip. Elevation gain: 2,140'
Approach: From Jeffersonville, drive north on Route 109, turn right on Route 118, and park where the Long Trail crosses the highway, near the height of land.

Belvidere Mountain   Jared Gange

97 **Prospect Rock 1,040'**

This is an easy, popular hike just west of Johnson village. Starting at the parking area on Hogback Road just off Route 15, it is a short road walk up to the Ithiel Falls Camp Meeting grounds. Here the Long Trail takes a right up a gravel driveway before bearing left into the forest. The trail starts with easy grades that become somewhat steeper as the trail winds its way up to Prospect Rock. The rock ledge here gives good views south of the Lamoille Valley below and nearby hills. Return by the same route.

1–1.5 hours, 1.5 miles, elevation gain: 530'

Approach: From Johnson, drive west 2.5 miles on Route 15 to Hogback Road. Bear right and park in the designated hiker area on the left side of the road.

98 Laraway Mountain 2,790'

Laraway Mountain is the highest summit along the crest of the Green Mountains between Route 15 (near Johnson) and Route 118. From the parking area at the end of Codding Hollow Road, take the Long Trail north. There is a good viewpoint at 2 miles with a very interesting view of Mount Mansfield, 15 miles to the south. The summit is reached at 2.4 miles. Descend by the same route.

3.5 hours and 4.8 miles round trip. Elevation gain: 1,550'
Approach: From Jeffersonville, drive north on Rt. 118 to Codding Hollow Rd., about 1.5 miles past Waterville. Follow it to the end (2.7 miles), staying left at 1.4 miles.

99 Mount Norris 2,575'

The Mount Norris Trail, maintained by the Mount Norris Boy Scout Reservation, follows logging roads and creek beds as it winds through hardwood forest, picking up various views before culminating in marvelous vistas of Belvidere Mountain, Jay Peak, and the landscape to the east and south. As the trail steepens you will encounter rock outcroppings until you reach the enjoyable final stroll on the wide ridge that continues to the summit. Return by the same route. Mount Norris lies to the east of the Long Trail and is not part of the Long Trail System.

2.5 hours and 3.6 miles, elevation gain: 1,300'
Approach: From Eden Mills, drive 2 miles north on Route 100. The trailhead is on the west side of the road, across from a Boy Scout camp.

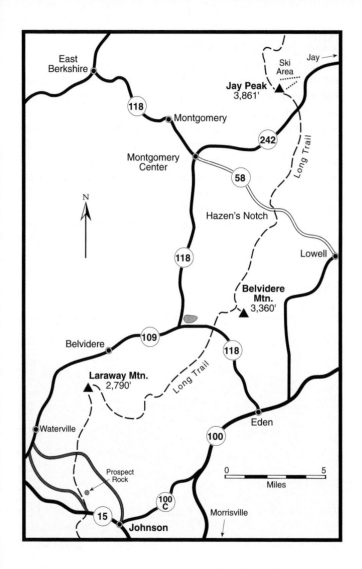

100 Jay Peak 3,861'

With a large tram station adjacent to the summit, Jay does not provide an unspoiled wilderness experience. However, this hike traverses a fine section of the Long Trail, and the views from the summit are superb. Take the Long Trail north from the parking area on Rt. 242. The rocky, well-maintained trail climbs briskly through birches and into the spruce-fir zone. Near the top, the trail crosses a ski trail before the final climb to the bare rock summit. Descend by the same route. It is also possible to climb Jay by one of the ski trails. The tram is in operation during the summer.

3 hours and 3.4 miles round trip. Elevation gain: 1,680'
Approach: From Montgomery Center, drive 6.8 miles north on Route 242 (or 5 miles south from the village of Jay) and park at the trail head parking, just south of the height of land.

Jay Peak from Troy, Vt.   David Seaver

Just to the south of Jay Peak, a 7-mile portion of the Long Trail makes for a good day hike. It is about 4 hours walking from Hazen's Notch to Route 242. From Hazen's Notch, head north on the Long Trail, passing Hazen's Notch Camp after a half mile, before beginning a steep climb. The summit of **Buchanan Mountain** (2,940') is reached at 4 miles, with a good view of Jay Peak. **Chet's Lookout** (at 4.2 miles) and **Domey's Dome** (at 5.2 miles) have good views as well. At 7 miles, the Long Trail crosses Route 242 and begins its ascent of Jay Peak, and Montgomery Center is about 6.5 miles away by road. To reach Hazen's Notch, follow Hazen's Notch Road 5.5 miles from Montgomery Center.

***Maps:** USGS Hazen's Notch, Jay Peak and DeLorme Atlas, pages 46, 52-53.*

Happy hikers on the summit!   Jared Gange

15 Hiking in Québec

The Canadian province of Québec is Vermont's nearest neighbor to the north. Although in general not as mountainous as Vermont, there are several mountain groups just across the border, in the area known as the **Eastern Townships**, that are definitely worth a visit. Mont Sutton, Mont Orford and Owl's Head — each a popular skiing destination as well — are only a short drive from Newport or Jay Peak. Larger than Alaska (about sixty times the size of Vermont), Québec offers fantastic opportunities for exploration. The St. Lawrence River regions of the Gaspé Peninsula, Saguenay Fjord, and Charlevoix are a few of the better-known destinations.

Owl's Head 2,450' (757m)

Rising abruptly from **Lake Memphremagog**, Owl's Head offers the most exciting mountain vantage point in the region. From the summit, views extend far into Quebec and south into Vermont, and beautiful 30-mile long Lake Memphremagog lies at your feet, 1,800' below. Typically hikers start at the base lodge (north side) and follow one of the ski trails to the top. For the most direct route, start at the main chair lift and follow the wide, grassy run straight to the summit. As you make your way upward, you will find small plateaus at each trail junction. These areas make an excellent place to take a rest and enjoy the views of Lake Memphremagog. From the top of the main chairlift, bear to the right on a side trail a short distance to a stairway on your left. Take the stairs and follow the trail alongside the power box up to the radio tower and the summit. Views from the summit are partially obscured by trees; a little exploring reveals some good lookout points. Views include

Owl's Head from steamer on Lake Memphremagog
19th century illustration from "Picturesque America"

Lake Memphremagog to the east, Round Top Mountain to the west of the lake, and Vermont's peaks to the south. Descend by the same route or, be adventurous and try one of the side trails on your way back to the parking area.

2.5 hours and 3 miles round trip. Gain 1,400'
Approach: From Mansonville, follow signs 6 miles (10 kilometers) east to Vale Perkins and Owl's Head Ski Area parking lot (the second entrance). Mansonville is on Québec route 243, a few miles into Canada from the North Troy border crossing.

Mont Orford 2,792' (853m)

The centerpiece of Mont Orford Provincial Park, Mont Orford, can be approached three ways. The most interesting route — and the longest — is the rugged northern ridge, which traverses Pic du Lynx and Mont Alfred DesRochers before reaching Orford's summit at 11 kilometers (ca. 6.6 miles) from the road. (The shortest route up Orford is from the base of the ski area.) From the park road (2 miles past Le Cerisier), follow Sentier de l'Estrie south 300 meters to the Castor shelter. About 300 meters farther on, the "les cretes" variation branches off (right) to begin its ascent of the north ridge. (Sentier de l'Estrie heads left over much easier ground on cross country ski trails, reaching the base of the ski area after 4 km. This provides the basis for a loop option with an easier and shorter — by 5 miles — return route.) The ridge route involves a great deal of steep climbing; in places ladders are used. The trail winds up through boulders and over rock outcrops, treating you to panoramic views from time to time. Bear Mountain, at 3 miles, offers a spectacular vista. The summit area of Mont Alfred-Desrochers has good lookouts, and finally, Mont Orford itself has a splendid view of the surrounding area.

22 kilometers (13 miles) round trip.
Elevation gain: approx. 1,000 meters (ca. 3,300')
Approach: Mount Orford is located near the town of Magog. From Autoroute 10 (exit 115), take Route 141 north for 3.5 miles. Turn left at the park administration building and continue 0.7 mile on the park road to the Le Cerisier recreation center.

Mont Sutton 3,182' (962m)

Mont Sutton is a provincial park and a major ski area. The Parc d'Environment Naturel de Sutton ("Parc Sutton") administers the area. For a spectacular view of the surrounding area, make the climb up popular Roundtop ("Sommet Rond" in French), the highest point of Mont Sutton. From the parking area, backtrack about 100m to a small green booth that marks the beginning of the trail. Follow the stairs and take a right at the first junction. The trail begins climbing after a bridge over a stream. It continues with moderate climbs followed by short flats at the frequent trail junctions. The trail is well-marked; however, keep in mind there are many trail junctions. Be sure to follow the correct path. The Alt 775 junction has a bench, an ideal spot to take a break. A side trip will take you to Lake Spruce, 700m distant. At the Alt 860 junction, the trail merges with the Eastern Trail. From here, the trail climbs more steeply the final 600m to the top. The summit area offers good views of the valley to the south and of Owl's Head to the east. Descending by the same route, the trail also provides a decent look at Lake Memphremagog. It's a quick 2.5 kilometers back to the parking area.

2 hours, 30 minutes and 3 miles (5km) round trip. Gain 1,450' (442m)

Approach: From Richford, Vermont, drive north on Route 139 into Canada and continue to the town of Sutton. Turn right on Maple Street and follow signs for Mont Sutton Ski Area. Continue on this road and bear left at the information center. Park at the Alt 520 (altitude 520 meters) lot at the end of the road.

The Eastern Trail

Les Sentiers de l'Estrie, in English, **The Eastern Trail**, is a 150-kilometer (90-mile) hiking trail in southern Québec, similar to Vermont's Long Trail. Starting near the hamlet of Glen Sutton, just across the border from Richford, Vermont, it traverses the high points of Mont Glen Sutton, Mont Sutton and Mont Orford before continuing to Kingsbury, about 20 miles northwest of Sherbrooke. The Trail, which is divided into seven sections, is accessible at a number of points at road crossings or by side trails. There are various designated camping sites along the way as well as simple shelters in Sutton Park and Orford Park (reservations required).

Most of the trail runs across private land, and the arrangement with the landowners requires all trail users to become members of the Sentiers de l'Estrie Club (20$ Can. for a family membership, guide book included). Having said that, the 25-km portion of the trail in **Mont Orford Provincial Park** is on public land, and hikers may use it for free.

Maps: The Sentiers de l'Estrie Club (P.O. Box 93, Sherbrooke, Québec J1H 5H5) publishes a detailed guide with nicely detailed maps. The booklet is available in English or in French.

The Montréal-based Québec Hiking Federation (Fédération Québecoise de la Marche) is a non-profit "mother organization" serving Québec hiking groups and individuals. For information on Les Sentiers de l'Estrie and other trails, you can contact the group at (514) 252-3157.

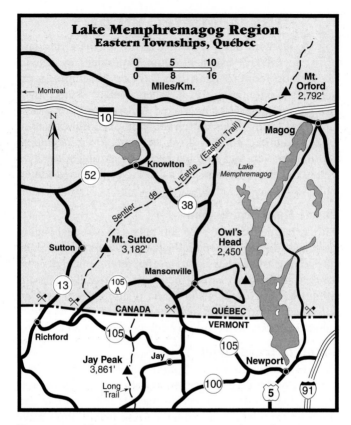

Lake Memphremagog Region
Eastern Townships, Québec

Topo maps: The Canadian government, through its Canada Map Office, Department of Energy, Mines, and Resources, provides a series of excellent topographic maps, similar to our USGS maps, at a scale of 1:50 000. The individual parks usually have simple, adequate hiking maps available for free.

16 Backcountry Skiing

With the rediscovery of the telemark turn and today's excellent equipment, skiers are able to handle most terrain. Hiking trails (on Camel's Hump, for example) are often used for an ascent, before skiing down through glades. And using waxed or "waxless" skis, skiers can cover many miles of terrain in good nordic fashion. While some backcountry areas are suitable for beginners (Little River, Nebraska Notch), skiers just starting out will do well to develop confidence at a touring center on groomed trails.

Mount Mansfield Region

With a trail network of over 200 miles, several challenging mountain traverses, steep and narrow alpine-style descents, miles of mellow woods skiing, and six interconnected cross country ski touring centers, the Stowe-Underhill-Jeff area is unequalled in New England. Some of the classic trips are described below, and the map shows in a general way how the backcountry trails and ski centers interconnect.

Bolton to Trapps Trail

This challenging tour from Bolton Valley Ski Area to Stowe is probably the classic backcountry ski tour in Vermont. It can be done in either direction but has less climbing and much better telemarking when starting from Bolton. After leaving the Bolton ski area, you pass through a glade of birches, contour across the face of Bolton Mountain, and finally descend 2,000' into Nebraska Valley. There are good views of Cottonbrook Basin and south to Camel's Hump along the way. Continue to Trapps via the Old County Road to Russell Knoll and follow signs to the Trapp ski shop.

20 km, 4–7 hours. A demanding tour in remote terrain.

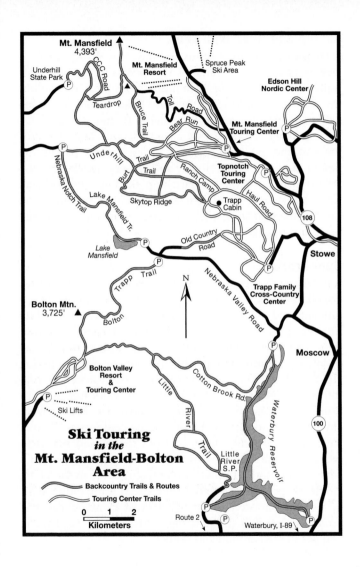

Ski Touring
in the
Mt. Mansfield-Bolton
Area

〰 Backcountry Trails & Routes
〰 Touring Center Trails

0   1   2
Kilometers

Skytop and Burt Trail Loop

A favorite, this route ascends and traverses Skytop Ridge to Dewey Saddle. It offers good viewpoints from short spur trails. Traveling a unique, high place in beautiful hardwoods, the trail starts (left) from the **Haul Road**, below the **Trapp Cabin**, just past the turnoff to Slayton Pasture. Initial steepness gradually gives way to an undulating climb. Towards the end, the trail works its way through dense balsam firs before dropping very steeply into **Dewey Saddle** and the Burt Trail. To finish the standard loop, ski down the Burt Trail (good glade skiing), and then take a right (sign; red markers) on the **Underhill Trail**, which traverses relatively easy terrain back to the Haul Road, completing the 2- to 3-hour loop.

Burt Trail

A telemarker's dream in powder, the upper section is worth the climb to get there. Up here, the hardwood forest is magnificent, and you will get to see some really huge white birches, trees that were too remote for loggers to bother with. The Burt drops a total of about 1,800' from **Dewey Saddle** into **Ranch Valley**, with the upper section offering about 800 to 900 feet of vertical. Most skiers access it from the Mount Mansfield Ski Touring Center, located just off Route 108. (See the description above for access from Skytop Ridge and Trapps.) From the ski center (pay the trail fee), ski on groomed trails (consult the posted maps) to where the Burt Trail leaves the ski area and turns into a backcountry trail. From this point (sign), settle in for a long climb (be prepared to find it untracked) using either skins or waxed skis. After about 500 feet of climbing you will cross the **Underhill Trail**, and once you reach Dewey Saddle, you get to turn around and ski down!

Cold conditions on a traverse of Camel's Hump   J. Gange

Overland and Underhill Trails

Linking Underhill with the Trapp and Mt. Mansfield touring centers, this important route lets you ski from the Burlington side of Mansfield to Stowe. Generally of moderate difficulty (it is a traverse, basically), it does cross some very steep terrain between the Long Trail and the Burt Trail. Prevailing snow conditions can make a huge difference in difficulty. (Note: There is a designated winter parking area near Maple Valley Farm; winter users should park here. This places you about a mile from the usual summer parking at the end of Stevensville Road.

From the Stevensville Road parking area, head up the hiking trail to Nebraska Notch, and after about 150 yards, veer left on the Overland Trail, probably unmarked. The trail climbs quite gradually at first, then moderately, as it uses switchbacks to gain altitude. During times of lean snow-cover the various stream crossings may pose a problem, especially on your descent, so bear this in mind.

Once you pass over the ridge — you will cross the Long Trail probably without noticing it — the Overland Trail branches left and descends to the Mansfield Ski Touring trail system, while the Underhill Trail begins a descending traverse of the very steep northern flank of Dewey Mountain. While there are no sustained, steep descents, a number of tricky places have to be negotiated, and intermediate skiers will find themselves out of their depth no matter what the ski conditions. The terrain eases as you approach the Burt Trail, and after crossing the Burt, things get downright easy all the way to the Haul Road on the Trapp trail system. Bear right on the Haul Road about 1 km. to reach the cabin.

About 3-5 hours from Stevensville parking to Trapps; recommended for advanced skiers.

The Great Trail Blazer leads the way   Louis Borie

CCC Road

This route gives you a chance to see up close the imposing west side of Mount Mansfield. From the gate at Underhill State Park (or lower down, depending on current snow conditions), ski up the graded CCC Road for 2 miles to its end. This road is generally excellent for intermediate level skiers. 7 km. roundtrip, 2–3 hours. Moderately easy, although it can be rutted and icy. The hiking trails on Mansfield are generally much too steep and narrow to offer any skiing enjoyment. Near its upper end, the CCC Road crosses the Teardrop Trail, a popular ski trail which drops off the summit ridge of Mansfield near the Nose. See page 140 for a description of the Teardrop.

Maps: *Northern Vermont Adventure Skiing*

Nebraska Notch Trail

From the parking area at the end of Stevensville road (snow conditions usually require parking lower down at the winter parking area), take the Nebraska Notch hiking trail up a gentle climb and across easy terrain to the beaver ponds at the base of impressive Nebraska Notch. A popular 4-mile round trip for beginner and intermediate skiers.

Little River State Park

A bit farther afield — it is approached from Waterbury — the Little River area contains a network of trails and old roads in generally moderate terrain, i.e. great nordic skiing. The large reservoir (popular with ice fishermen) offers a complete change from steep, wooded trails. The main route from the dam through to Moscow (groomed for snowmobiles) is excellent and can be combined with skiing the length of the reservoir for a great loop that takes 3 to 5 hours. Use extreme caution on the reservoir, especially near streams and along the shoreline.

Teardrop Trail (west side of Mt. Mansfield)

The area's classic ski descent plunges off Mansfield's summit ridge. Steep and very narrow at the top, the trail widens and the terrain moderates as you descend. It can be approached from above by riding the lift to the Octagon (Mt. Mansfield Ski Area) and skiing up and over the summit ridge on the TV Road (continuation of the Toll Road), but most ski up the **CCC Road** to where it intersects the Teardrop, or they pick up the Lower Teardrop from Underhill State Park. You will need climbing skins for this ascent. Easily picked out from Underhill Center, the Teardrop Trail appears as a thin white line just north of Maple Ridge. **Difficulty rating: Expert.**

Bruce Trail

Although a less serious undertaking than Teardrop, the Bruce Trail is still a challenging run requiring quick reflexes. Beginning from the Octagon (take the lift), it drops 2,000' into Ranch Valley, merging with the Overland Trail (cross country ski trail, Mt. Mansfield Touring Center) after a mile.

Honey Hollow (Camel's Hump north side)

This north-facing basin is a favorite section of the Catamount Trail. As it is in somewhat remote terrain, and the initial part of the descent has steep, narrow sections, the tour is advanced. Usually accessed from Camel's Hump Nordic Ski Center in Huntington from the top of Logger's Loop ski run, the 5-mile trail descends 1,600' to the Winooski River in Jonesville. It is easier to ski up the trail and then back to your car. Park on River Rd., 2.5 miles east of the Jonesville bridge.

Huntington Gap

The full version of this long tour starts from Mad River Barn (Waitsfield), ascends Phenn Basin, and crosses the main ridge of the Green Mountains, before dropping steeply out of Huntington Gap and commencing a long northerly traverse above Huntington Valley (at about 1,500'), reaching Camel's Hump Nordic Ski Center after 15 miles. A 6-mile version of the route is to bail out at the first opportunity on the Huntington side, in Hanksville. Huntington Gap can be done as an out-and-back trip by using the excellent snowmobile trail from the end of Trapp Road, above Huntington Center.

Catamount Ski Trail

The Catamount Trail is the Vermont end-to-end cross country ski trail that roughly parallels the Long Trail. Conceived in 1982, the Catamount Trail is still under development, with the route not finalized in some areas. By the winter of 2001-2, about 95 percent of the 300 miles will be available for use. The Catamount Trail is generally at much lower elevations than the Long Trail. Thus, instead of running along the high ridges of the Green Mountains, it seeks out skiable backcountry routes, which link the various ski centers together. For example, from below Middlebury Gap, the route runs north on unplowed roads over Lincoln Gap, then near the bases of the Sugarbush and Mad River ski areas, before again crossing the main ridge. It then continues north along the west flank of Camel's Hump to Bolton Valley Ski Area and on to the Trapp trail ski in Stowe. The member-supported (1,500 members) **Catamount Trail Association**, based in Burlington, publishes the **Catamount Trail Guidebook**.

Blueberry Hill to Breadloaf

A 9.5-mile ski over moderate, gently rolling terrain from Goshen to Ripton, the trail is done in either direction or as a round trip, and it is a very accessible and popular segment of the Catamount Trail. This ski runs from the cross country ski area at the Blueberry Hill Inn to the Rickert Ski Center (Breadloaf campus) on Route 125, a short distance from Middlebury. This is an excellent trail for skiers wanting to try out the backcountry. South of Blueberry Hill, the trail continues to Goshen. A variation through Leicester Hollow takes you directly to the Churchill House Inn on Route 73 in Goshen.

Somerset Reservoir

This relatively remote section of the Catamount Trail runs along the east shore of Somerset Reservoir, deep in the Green Mountain National Forest. From the parking on Kelley Stand Road (south of Stratton Mountain), the trail heads south on the access road to Grout Pond, passing the pond to the west. Continuing south, it soon reaches Somerset Reservoir and runs along its east side, reaching the dam (and access road) at the south end, for a total distance of 7.5 miles. The Grout Pond area has a network of ski trails, and a cabin is available for winter users.

Hazen's Notch-Jay Pass Area

Skiing through Hazen's Notch on unplowed Bailey Hazen Military Road (Route 58) has long been a favorite ski tour in the north country. After the fine and fast 500' descent from Hazen's Notch (elev. 1,800'), the trail leads to Hazen's Notch Nordic Center. Continuing north, there is excellent skiing up to Jay Pass where there are good views. From the pass, a fine, rolling descent to Jay village awaits you.

Beaver Meadow Trail

A little north of Stowe, the Sterling Brook-Mud City area offers some good backcountry skiing of moderate difficulty, and the Catamount Trail passes through the area. To do the ca. 10 km. roundtrip to Beaver Meadow Lodge, park at the end of Beaver Meadow Road (it branches off Mud City Road) and follow the hiking trail to the lodge, making the loop around the beaver pond. Beaver Meadow Lodge is nestled at the base of the steep east flank of Morse Mountain; Smugglers Notch Ski Area is on the opposite side of the mountain. Those looking for a little extra workout can check out the glades just to the south of the lodge.

Onion River Sports

20 Langdon Street
Montpelier
229-9409

SKI, BIKE & OUTDOOR STORE

BACKPACKS • TENTS • SLEEPING BAGS
STOVES • HIKING BOOTS • OUTDOOR CLOTHING
KINGDOM TRAIL MAPS & INFO
ACCESSORIES & FRIENDLY SERVICE

ROUTE 114, EAST BURKE VILLAGE, VT 05832
(802) 626-3215

Index

Useful organizations: Phone numbers and websites

Green Mountain Club
802-244-7037 www.greenmountainclub.org
Vermont Department of Forests, Parks and Recreation
802-241-3655 www.vtstateparks.com
Green Mountain National Forest
802-747-6700 www.fs.fed.us/r9/gmfl
Vermont Department of Tourism and Marketing
www.1-800-vermont.com
Appalachian Trail Conference
304-535-6331 www.atconf.org
Vermont Youth Conservation Corps
800-639-8922 www.vycc.org
Mount Mansfield State Forest
802-479-3241
Craftsbury Outdoor Center
800-729-7751 www.craftsbury.com
Merck Forest and Farmland
802-394-7836 www.merckforest.com
Catamount Trail Association
802-864-5794 www.catamounttrail.org
Great Outdoor Recreation Page (GORP)
www.gorp.com
New England Outdoor Activities
www.neoactivities.com/hiking

About the Author

Jared Gange has hiked and cross country skied in New England and the Adirondacks for 15 years. He has hiked and climbed in the Cascades, the Rockies, the Alps, Norway, Pakistan, Tibet and Nepal. He has previously written several hiking guides for New Hampshire, Vermont and the Northeast.